D0457702

I have known Lenya Heitzig and her husband, Skip, for many years, and I know her passion for seeking God in every aspect of life. Lenya and Skip have traveled with me in my work at Samaritan's Purse, and I have watched firsthand as she has discovered "holy moments" in unexpected places. This book encourages all of us to do the same by keeping the eyes of our heart focused on Christ.

FRANKLIN GRAHAM
PRESIDENT AND CEO
BILLY GRAHAM EVANGELISTIC ASSOCIATION
SAMARITAN'S PURSE

It is often difficult to recognize God in the mundane, and yet that is where He often meets us. My friend Lenya Heitzig gives us practical, concrete ways that we can cultivate the holy in the ordinary, turning it into the extraordinary.

RUTH GRAHAM
BEST-SELLING AUTHOR
PRESIDENT, RUTH GRAHAM AND FRIENDS

In our increasingly secular, skeptical culture, *Holy Moments* is a must-read! Thank you, Lenya Heitzig, for helping me keep my eyes open . . . for Him . . . everywhere!

ANNE GRAHAM LOTZ
FOUNDER AND PRESIDENT OF ANGEL MINISTRIES

Here's a reviving wake-up call! After reading
Holy Moments, I suddenly understood how God has been
communicating to me all these years by placing me in
circumstances that I thought were . . . well, just
coincidence. Now I know better, and I'm looking forward
to experiencing more encounters of God's providence.

JOSH MCDOWELL
AUTHOR AND SPEAKER

The power behind this book is not just in the concepts, the
stories and the illustrations—although they are important.
It is in the authentic life of the author, which makes this
book unique. In a world of superficial Christianity, it is truly
refreshing to read a book like *Holy Moments* that can help us
touch God and experience His life in our daily walk. This
could very well be the answer to your question, How can
I experience more of God in my life?

DR. K. P. YOHANNAN
INTERNATIONAL PRESIDENT, GOSPEL FOR ASIA

MOMENTS

LENYA HEITZIG

Regal

From Gospel Light
Ventura, California, U.S.A.

PUBLISHED BY REGAL BOOKS
FROM GOSPEL LIGHT
VENTURA, CALIFORNIA, U.S.A.
PRINTED IN THE U.S.A.

Regal Books is a ministry of Gospel Light, a Christian publisher dedicated to serving the local church. We believe God's vision for Gospel Light is to provide church leaders with biblical, user-friendly materials that will help them evangelize, disciple and minister to children, youth and families.

It is our prayer that this Regal book will help you discover biblical truth for your own life and help you meet the needs of others. May God richly bless you.

For a free catalog of resources from Regal Books/Gospel Light, please call your Christian supplier or contact us at 1-800-4-GOSPEL *or* www.regalbooks.com.

Library of Congress Cataloging-in-Publication Data
Heitzig, Lenya.
 Holy moments / Lenya Heitzig.
   p. cm.
 ISBN 0-8307-4287-5 (hard cover)
 1. Christian life. I. Title.
 BV4501.3.H44 2006
 248.4—dc22   2006025211

1   2   3   4   5   6   7   8   9   10   /   10   09   08   07   06

Rights for publishing this book in other languages are contracted by Gospel Light Worldwide, the international nonprofit ministry of Gospel Light. Gospel Light Worldwide also provides publishing and technical assistance to international publishers dedicated to producing Sunday School and Vacation Bible School curricula and books in the languages of the world. For additional information, visit www.gospellightworldwide.org; write to Gospel Light Worldwide, P.O. Box 3875, Ventura, CA 93006; or send an e-mail to info@gospellightworldwide.org.

Contents

Foreword

Have you ever had an experience that renews your wonder at God's love for you? Or do these holy moments pass you by undetected and unappreciated? Too often, we are like the two disciples on the road to Emmaus (see Luke 24:13-16). We don't recognize that the Lord Himself has come to walk along beside us.

Holy moments can happen at any time—even on summer days in Riverside, California. I remember a sultry afternoon when the breeze had finally begun to stir the air. I was a young mother who had finally succeeded in getting my young son to lie down for a late nap. I took refuge on the porch swing to let my thoughts wander. Dangling my legs, I watched the shadows lengthen across the lawn.

Just then, I spied something small popping up and down over in the deep grass. I wondered, *What is that?* It was nothing special—just a little brown bird, pecking busily on the ground. Amused, I watched as it flew across the lawn, and landed on another spot.

It lured me off the porch. But as I approached, it flew up into the branches of a tree. Down the street, a young couple had also been watching the bird. As they and their two small daughters strolled to a stop, the mother said with a smile, "Hello, I'm Karen."

She looked to be about my age, with long brown hair, freckles and deep blue eyes. One of the girls looked just like her mom, the other resembled her dad. I smiled back and said, "Hi, I'm Cathe."

"I recognize you. You're Cathe Laurie, aren't you?"

"Uhhh . . . yes, I am," I replied.

"We go to your church," she said excitedly. "Would you like to come over and have lunch sometime? We just live a few streets over."

I was only 22 years old and a new pastor's wife. Our church was a growing congregation of mostly young families. My antennae went up. I wondered, *Is she lonely, new to the community, or just plain desperate?* I recognized the familiar look that a young mother gets on her face. The "*help me, I need to talk about grown-up things*" look.

A few days later, I went to her home for lunch—ordinary peanut butter and jelly on whole wheat, surprisingly served on her Great Aunt Ann's elegant china. Karen had a way of making ordinary things seem special. Unfortunately, as we began to get acquainted, my son Christopher and her daughter Ericka decided to torment and tattle on each other. As we said our goodbyes, she suggested we try it again. I thought, *She's really nice, but this isn't working with the kids.*

Thankfully, we did meet again and discovered that we had more in common than strong-willed children and the need for grown-up conversation. We were the original "desperate housewives." We were desperate for meaningful dialogue; but more than that, we had a hunger to learn and develop our faith in the Lord.

One day Karen said, "Cathe, there are so many women like us at Harvest Christian Fellowship. You should begin a Bible study for them." Though I did not feel equipped to lead a women's ministry, she inspired me to try. "I'll help you," she added. And she did!

You may have seen the bumper sticker, "Lord, help me to be the person my dog thinks I am." That summed up my unspoken prayer, *Lord, make me the person Karen thinks I am.* God gave me a gift in my dear friend; she was a godly servant who came alongside to join me and help launch a women's ministry that has touched thousands of lives.

It is sheer joy to stand back and see the fruit of those early years. Together, we laughed and cried, prayed and planned, decorated and discovered ways to work out a dream of helping women grow in Christ.

Though I didn't realize it at the time, the Lord used that little bird in the grass to draw us together in a life-long friendship. And why not? He used ravens to feed Elijah, a whale to redirect Jonah, a donkey to save Balaam's life, and a fish to provide for Peter's taxes! And I am *still* amused at how God can use such small things in wholly, *holy* unexpected ways to alter the course of our lives. The Lord has used Lenya's book to remind me of the holy moments I have already experienced and to challenge me to be on the look-out for more of God's fingerprints in my future. I pray that as you peruse these pages, you will find God's handiwork in the midst of your ordinary happenstance.

Cathe Laurie
Wife of Greg Laurie
Director of Harvest Women's Ministry

Introduction

....

It's easy to find evidence of God in the midst of extraordinary circumstances. It's not so easy to detect Him during the ordinary events in our lives. But that's exactly where you and I live. Most of us will never walk on water, heal the sick or cast out demons. But we may provide a meal for the needy, offer encouragement to the downhearted or receive an answer to one of our prayers.

We live amidst the nuance of the normal with God's voice echoing somewhere off in the distance, not thundering from the mountain peaks. That is precisely the reason we need to be sensitive to His quiet voice and gentle leading, to the holy moments we often overlook as we rush madly through our daily routines.

This book will help you become aware of the more subtle ways that God works and amplify your spiritual sensitivity to His inescapable presence. Nineteenth-century Scottish theologian James Denney wrote, "The important thing in religion is not to believe that God is omniscient but to experience that God knows me. The important thing is not that God is everywhere but that wherever I am, God is with me."

Heaven Sent

Nothing seemed out of the ordinary that bright Sunday morning as I jogged down the same route I had taken the previous six days of my vacation in Honolulu. It was a picture-postcard day in paradise. As I ran, I passed surfers catching blue-green waves that would eventually crash and subside on the sandy shores of Waikiki. I followed a course past touristy Kalakaua Avenue, through exotic Kapiolani Park and up the stark volcanic slopes of Diamond Head.

Suddenly, trouble in paradise hit hard. *Ouch*! At the halfway point of a five-mile excursion, I stopped dead in my tracks. The mother of all charley horses gripped my left calf—I was paralyzed with pain. Stumbling, then fumbling for a nearby wall, I did every conceivable stretch in a desperate attempt to loosen the unrelenting cramp. Nothing worked. I was two-and-a-half miles away from my hotel with no money for a taxi, so I began hobbling toward my final destination.

After navigating several blocks in agonizing discomfort, God tapped me on the shoulder—or should I say, spoke to my heart: *Lenya, why don't you pray?*

Why didn't I think of that sooner? Then I asked Him, "Lord, help! I can't make it back without damaging my leg further. Please send me help or heal me. What should I do?"

Through the park, strewn with palm trees and fragrant plumeria blossoms, I spotted a bright banner stretched across a minibus: *Heaven Sent.* I smiled at God's sense of humor and

His impeccable timing. What was that minibus doing smack-dab in my path? Should I limp up and knock on the window?

Then the rest of the sign came into focus: *Heaven Sent— Mobile Massage Therapy*. "This is too good to be true," I mumbled. Then I wondered, *Could this be a holy moment orchestrated by God's good hand?*

Just then a local named Bunny Gabaylo stepped out to ask if I needed help. A pleading request tumbled out of my mouth. "I've just injured myself running. I've got two more miles to go. Could you work out the knot in my calf? The problem is, I'm not carrying any money to pay you."

He simply handed me a flyer, and said in Pidgin English, "It your lucky day. I offering two-minute massage free to first-time customer."

Bunny, a licensed massage therapist, worked on my calf for nearly 20 minutes applying shiatsu acupressure, deep-tissue massage and Tiger Balm. While I lay on the padded exam table, listening to Julio Iglesias over the high-tech sound system, Bunny graciously offered his healing touch. When I noticed a picture of Jesus on the wall of his minibus, I said, "Are you a Christian?"

He affirmed that he was and added, "I should be at church, since it Sunday. But a friend invite me to Kapiolani Park for race that end here today." When I stood up, I was overjoyed to discover that my gait had straightened out and my leg was greatly improved. I thanked him and offered to send a check in payment for his services. But Bunny refused, saying, "This my calling. No charge for you."

The next two miles seemed more like two blocks as I delighted myself in the Lord who had granted me the desires of my heart by answering my prayer the precise moment it was uttered. I asked God for help during a time of need and He provided an answer that was truly *heaven-sent*!

The divinely appointed meeting with Bunny was not my first holy moment, and God has showered me with many other such moments since then. All these events have convinced me that they are available to anyone, from unbelievers to those who are passionate about following God—and He can send holy moments to many people simultaneously. Holy moments are God's subtle way of getting our attention. They serve as a sweet reminder that He is near.

I am not more special than anyone else—our heavenly Father doesn't play favorites. However, I've developed a sensitivity to holy moments because of a Scripture that became my life's verse many years ago.

> Delight yourself also in the LORD, and He shall give you the desires of your heart. Commit your way to the LORD, trust also in Him, and He shall bring it to pass (Ps. 37:4-5).

Meditating upon Psalm 37:4-5 opened my eyes to the ways that God moves among us. He longs to intersect our paths with His heavenly interruptions. If you will apply the godly guidelines found throughout the rest of this book, you'll develop the ability to identify the holy moments from your past as well as recognize more of them in the future.

In the remainder of this book, we'll explore the five phrases found in Psalm 37:4-5 that represent five simple steps. They are

- Delight in the Holy One
- Develop holy desires
- Dedicate your direction
- Depend wholly on Him
- Discover holy moments

The five pearls of wisdom extracted from this passage can radically impact your Christian journey with incredible moments of divine inspiration and intervention. Each chapter includes examples of holy moments from my own life as well as from the lives of others. And every lesson concludes with a prayer to encourage you to draw closer to your Creator and open your eyes to recognize God's loving intervention in your life.

CHAPTER ONE

Defining Holy Moments

*God's invisible qualities—his eternal power and
divine nature—have been clearly seen.*

ROMANS 1:20, *NIV*

Sherlock Holmes fingered crooks by investigating the footprints they left behind. The size, the tread pattern and the depth of the print revealed pertinent clues, such as the height, weight or occupation of the perpetrator. You can imagine the famous sleuth saying, "If the shoe fits the crime scene, it's elementary, my dear Watson." Modern detectives now use fingerprints to identify lawbreakers.

Why? Because no two fingerprints have ever been found to be alike in billions of human and automated computer comparisons. Among other accomplishments, Sir Francis Galton (1822-1911) devised a method for classifying fingerprints that are used in forensics today. He calculated that the odds of two individual fingerprints being the same were 1 in 64 billion. Even identical twins have different thumbprints.

Over time, most visible human characteristics change; fingerprints do not. Amazingly, if you injure the tip of your finger, your skin will grow back in the same pattern—once the skin heals, your original fingerprint remains.

That's why, for thousands of years, fingerprints have been used to identify individuals. The ancient Chinese and Assyrians used fingerprints on legal documents. The ancient kings of Babylon would press their entire right hand into a slab of clay embedded with a decree before it was enacted. Today we leave our thumbprint beside our signature when we sign important legal and financial documents.

It's fun to imagine that God has fingerprints too. Wouldn't it be amazing to trace His identity by the marks He leaves behind? Moses claimed that the first set of the Ten Commandments was "written with the finger of God" (Exod. 31:18). Whatever that means, it stands to reason that if God has fingers, then surely He leaves fingerprints! I believe that holy moments are God's way of leaving fingerprints in His hope that we will discover His identity. Holy moments provide evidence of where He's been and what He's been doing. Through holy moments, God makes an unmistakable impression in our lives and points us toward heaven. The trick is to detect those holy moments.

I've become a sleuth, dusting for God's fingerprints in ordinary places, such as my kitchen, and in unexpected places, such as airplanes. I'm in pursuit of the One who has left proof of His existence in nature, evidence of His love through His Son, verification of the truth in His Word, and traces of His kindness in my life. I pray that you, too, will be inspired to become a clever detective who searches for and finds God's fingerprints.

God's Fingerprints

The greatest sleuth would have found it difficult to uncover God's fingerprints in a Nazi concentration camp. But that was the first place where a 12-year-old boy, Herman Rosenblat, would detect God's good hand. Interned with his two older brothers, Herman was expected to survive on one slice of bread per day. His siblings, concerned about their younger brother's development, sacrificed one-quarter of their single slice of bread to little Herman each day. He said, "When all you have to eat is one slice of bread and you break off a quarter for someone else? That's love."[1]

But Herman also experienced love through an unexpected hand, that of a nine-year-old girl, "who for months tossed apples and bread across a fence to help that little boy survive."[2] She lived near the camp and simply wanted to help the little boy on the other side of the fence. One day, however, Herman was transferred to another camp and believed that he would never see his tiny helper again.

Fourteen years later, while living in New York, a buddy coerced Herman into joining him on a blind date. Herman and his date discovered that they shared similar backgrounds as Polish immigrants. Herman eventually told her about his childhood in a concentration camp. Roma, his nervous date, told him that she used to live near a camp where she would sneak food across the fence each day to help a little boy.

"'That was me!' Rosenblat exclaimed. "Now that I have found you, I'm not going to ever let you go." He proposed marriage right on the spot. After six months of courtship, the couple married. As of 2006, they are still celebrating anniversaries together. Their rabbi, Anchelle Perl, said, "His whole story is about how the hand of God brought him and his Roma together after many years."[3]

Holy Moments

What is a holy moment? The words "holy moment" are not found in the *Merriam-Webster's* dictionary along with a list of hard-to-pronounce words or simple synonyms. A holy moment is best described as a supernatural surprise orchestrated by our loving Savior. It's God's way of letting His children know that He's there, He cares and He hears our prayers. Holy moments occur when we discover signs of the miraculous in the midst of a sea of the mundane, as God transforms our ordinary circumstances into extraordinary outcomes.

These circumstances may not include a burning bush, a thundering voice or bright lights from heaven. But they may include a timely phone call, an unforeseen roadblock, a caring word or being at the right place at the right time. When an unexpected turn of events causes you to realize that God loves you, that moment truly becomes holy.

Dissecting the Words

Let's pull these two words apart—"holy" and "moment"—and then put them back together again. As we do, we'll gain a greater understanding of how the divine intersects with our everyday experience.

First, what does "holy" mean? It's a term that refers to persons, places or things that are set apart or separated for God's special purpose. For instance, the seventh day, the Sabbath, was to be separate from every other day of the week—a holy day to commune with God. When Moses encountered the burning bush in the Sinai desert, God instructed him to go barefoot because the very ground he stood upon was holy, a sacred place where Moses encountered the Lord. In the Old Testament, any gifts or offerings presented to the Lord—from grain to goats—were consecrated, wholly dedicated to a holy God. Therefore, anyone or anything, anyplace or any time set apart for God becomes holy.

"Moment" is a word that describes a portion of, or point in, time. Because moments occur frequently, day-in and day-out, the tendency is to take them for granted. What is one more grain of sand passing through the hourglass of time? But have you ever had an experience when time stood still? When you seemed stuck in the moment or the moment stayed stuck on you?

Such instances define us. They create a demarcation be-

tween then and now—between before and after. In the blink
of an eye, nothing is the same. Those moments are forever set
apart from the multitude of moments that have come before
or will follow after.

Why does God sprinkle our paths with holy moments?
I believe they occur to remind us of His inescapable presence
(see Ps. 139:7-12). They offer us a glimpse of God. Holy moments are God's way of making Himself known. As a result,
they create a desire within us to know Him even better.
James, the brother of Jesus, wrote, "Draw near to God and He
will draw near to you" (Jas. 4:8). The Lord desires us to develop an ongoing, reciprocal relationship with Him. As a rela-
tional being, God possesses personality traits and emotions—
He has His likes and dislikes. Holy moments introduce us to
the different aspects of His unique personality.

Likewise, we long to be known by God for who we are.
We all hunger for significance. A holy moment can reveal
that God knows each of us by name (see John 10:3), has
numbered the hairs of our head (see Matt. 10:30), collects
our tears in a bottle (see Ps. 56:8), and understands the
unspoken cries of our heart (see Ps. 139). God desires a relationship with you and me that is not based on rote, ritual
or religion but on meaningful relationship. His call, "Adam,
where are you?" (see Gen. 3:9), still echoes in our ears today.
Holy moments are His way of beckoning us to come out
of hiding.

I believe that one of humankind's greatest needs is for intimacy—deep, meaningful companionship. My idea of intimacy centers on relationships in which we feel free to expose our true selves—to reveal the deepest part of our nature to another. Intimacy is marked by a warm friendship developed through long association. It's more than a superficial acquaintance. It's about loving others and being loved for who we really are.

Author Josh McDowell wrote, "I believe two of the greatest fears people struggle with today are the fear that they will never be loved and the fear that they will never be able to love. People are seeking meaningful, intimate and lasting relationships. I don't believe we've had a sexual revolution, rather, I believe we have experienced a revolution in search of intimacy."[4] It has been said that there's a God-shaped hole in all of us. Only the Lord can fill that gaping void. The psalmist confirms, "He satisfies the longing soul" (Ps. 107:9).

Describing the Experience

"Providence" is the unique word Christians have used throughout history to describe holy moments. Providence is God's subtle intervention in the affairs of humankind. When God's unseen hand orchestrates small details of your life to bring about startling outcomes, that holy moment is evidence of His providence.

Some skeptics would call providence coincidence. However, as Bill Moyers has astutely commented, "Coincidence is God's way of remaining anonymous."[5] In other words, providence is God incognito—a situation in which He leaves His fingerprints without revealing His hand. These situations may not involve parted seas, manna from heaven or a star in the sky to guide your way. But they could mean a life-changing meeting or finding yourself with the exact resources to help someone in need. No two fingerprints left by the hand of God are identical.

I have a friend who is always looking for divine revelation, a moment of lucid illumination that will shine holy insight into her befuddled world. She likes to call these unexpected bursts of insight "Aha!" moments. These are times of keen awareness into a hidden truth or the surprising realization that something has divine significance. Aha! moments occur when your life suddenly makes "sense" in the truest meaning of the word.

Ancient humankind called these moments of clarity an epiphany, which simply means "to make manifest or show more." Therefore, when you see something you've never seen before or discover a truth that unlocks an unsolved mystery, you are having an epiphany—what I call a holy moment.

Throughout history, different terminology has been used to describe out-of-the-ordinary experiences. But as Shakespeare said, "That which we call a rose by any other name would smell as sweet." So call them what you will—providence, Aha! moments, epiphanies, synchronicity or serendipity—they are all evidence of the unseen hand of God creating holy moments out of the seemingly happenstance events of our lives. And they occur in order to point us to God, the holy One.

For a Christian, there's no such thing as luck. Believing

that fate has dealt you a good or bad hand denies God's hand of providence in your life.

I do not trust the austere hands of fate with my future. Instead, I rely on a loving God who orchestrates circumstances that are favorable or unfavorable, according to His will for me. When difficult situations arise, I ponder, *Am I in the will of God? Have I been obedient to His Word?* or *Is the Lord redirecting my path?* When favorable circumstances come my way, I count them as God's blessings—as His affirmation that I'm on the right track. Yet I know that whether good or bad things happen, God will work all things together for my good and His glory (see Rom. 8:28).

Late for Practice

When I was a brand-new Christian, I loved hearing about the extraordinary events that happened in the lives of ordinary people like you and me. One of my favorite real-life tales took place in Beatrice, Nebraska. The story begins in a little church called West Side Baptist that was known for its choir. Like clockwork, the choir members practiced at church every Wednesday night at precisely 7:20 P.M. But on March 1, 1950, everyone had an excuse for being late, from the sopranos to the basses.

Marilyn Paul, the church pianist, fell asleep after dinner, so she and her mother were late. Ladonna Vandergrift, a high school sophomore, was having trouble with her homework, so she ran behind schedule. Slowed down by car trouble, a married couple that provided transportation for several other members of the choir meant that a whole carload would be delayed. Amazingly, 20 people, including every singer, the choir director, Reverend Walter Klempel and his wife, were all late. And all of them had excellent excuses. At precisely 7:25 P.M., the time when chorus rehearsal should have begun, not one soul was in the choir loft—and that had never happened before.

That peculiar night the church furnace ignited a gas leak in the basement of the West Side Baptist Church and the whole building burst into a blaze. The furnace room was right below the choir loft—where the choir should have been singing! The walls collapsed outward while the heavy roof crashed straight down in a deadfall. The blast forced a nearby radio station off the air and shattered windows in surrounding homes.

If Marilyn had been the only survivor, she might have assumed that there was nothing uncommon about an after-dinner snooze. (And personally, I've never thought car trouble constituted a miraculous turn of events). No high school student in his or her right mind would consider homework the handiwork of God. But on May 1, 1950, if you belonged to the choir at the West Side Baptist Church in Beatrice, Nebraska, the most ordinary excuse became extraordinary evidence of God's using everyday circumstance to accomplish His will.

Perhaps statisticians could calculate the exact odds of all

these random events occurring simultaneously, yet it seems safe to say that chances are one in a million that the entire choir would arrive late on the same evening! All these years later, the still-surviving members believe that their ordinary circumstances were an act of God.

Perhaps you've always assumed that supernatural surprises only happen to old, dead saints. That's not true! Holy moments take place in everyone's life—because holy moments are meant to point us to the Holy One. They are God's way of drawing back the curtains in heaven so that we can see Him moving behind the scenes and moving all the scenes that He's behind. When unbelievers experience holy moments, it is God's way of getting their attention too. He's showing them that He's in on the act and longs to be Director of all their tomorrows.

Birds in Flight

I enjoyed a "pre-saved" holy moment that gave me a glimpse of God as the author of life. Raised an atheist, as a sophomore in college, I was bothered by the conversion of my skeptical father to Christianity. Billy Graham's book *How to Be Born Again* was a best-seller that year, so I decided to purchase a copy to gain insight into my father's newfound faith. Spreading out a blanket on the shores of Lake Michigan, I pulled out my book for a leisurely read. An excerpt from chapter 3, "Does God Really Speak to Us?" made me blurt out loud, "Yeah, right!" Graham proposed that God was the

Creator who speaks to His creatures through creation: "In its own language, nature speaks of God's existence, whether it is the cry of a baby or the song of a meadowlark . . . the instincts of a bird are within his plans."[6]

Arrogantly, I decided to put Creator God to a test, challenging, "If You formed the instincts within a bird and want to show me that You are sovereign over all, then influence the bird tweeting in the distance to sing a little song for me by landing upon the tree I'm sitting under." Fluttering out of the distance, a small gray swallow came into view. Then he lit upon the branch above my head and chirped a happy melody. Closing the book ceremoniously, I thought, *Maybe God really does exist and has created me for a purpose.*

Just like that, in a holy moment, God had sprung the lock on a college coed's closed mind with His unseen hand of providence. I began attending Calvary Chapel in Costa Mesa, California, and two months later I offered my heart to the Lord. My experience is evidence that holy moments are designed to draw us closer to the Holy One.

God is creator of heaven and Earth, sovereign over all He has made. And His creations, from the stars at night to the birds in flight, are evidence of His divine nature. Paul tells us, "since the creation of the world God's invisible qualities—his eternal power and divine nature—have been clearly seen, being understood from what has been made, so that men are without excuse" (Rom. 1:20, *NIV*). Nothing, not even the fall or the flight of a sparrow, escapes God's all-seeing eye. And He uses the intricacies of nature to get the attention of His ultimate creation, humanity. People like you and me are much more valuable to God than a flock of sparrows (see Luke 12:7).

Holy Happenstance

In the Old Testament, we see how Ruth from Moab reaped her share of hard and happy circumstances. Before putting her faith in the God of Israel, she experienced poverty, scorn and loneliness when the husband of her youth died unexpectedly. But those unhappy occurrences compelled her to join her widowed mother-in-law, Naomi, on a journey of faith leading all the way to the Promised Land. "*Dis*-appointment" can be transformed into "*His*-appointment" with one small event. These two destitute widows arrived in Bethlehem just as famine burst into feasting—it was the beginning of the harvest.

Upon her arrival in Bethlehem, Ruth did not sulk in self-pity but went to work gleaning in the barley fields. At that time, landowners set aside crops growing in the corners of their fields, as well as anything missed on the first pass through the fields, for the poor to harvest. While Ruth was a part of ancient Israel's welfare system, and from human perspective she may have thought that she just "happened to come to the part of the field belonging to Boaz, who was of the family of [her father-in-law] Elimelech" (Ruth 2:3), from a heavenly point of view, God's hand of providence nudged her in the right direction—the perfect field to find grain and

a groom. Homespun Bible commentator J. Vernon McGee
wrote,

> If you'd seen Ruth going out down the road from Beth-
> lehem, you would have seen a girl who had no idea
> into which field she should go. . . . It's going to be
> very important that she get in that field. If she doesn't,
> then you tell the wise men that there's no use coming
> to Bethlehem. Jesus won't be born there. And you can
> tell the shepherds to stay with their flocks on the hill-
> side because He won't be born in Bethlehem. You see,
> it's important that she go into the right field.[7]

As if on cue, while Ruth labored in that very field, "behold,
Boaz came" (Ruth 2:4) on the scene. Immediately, the hand-
some landowner noticed Ruth and asked his servant who she
was. Upon hearing of her dedication and unselfish service to
Naomi, Boaz was love-struck. He invited her to stay in his
fields throughout the harvest season. Then he secretly did her
a favor: "And when she rose up to glean, Boaz commanded his
young men, saying, 'Let her glean even among the sheaves, and
do not reproach her. Also let grain from the bundles fall purposely for her; leave it that she may glean, and do not rebuke
her'" (Ruth 2:15-17).

Boaz left a trail of barley for Ruth to discover. The story
reveals that the trail led to his very heart. Eventually, Boaz
redeemed her from her desperate situation, and Ruth got a

second chance at life. After a dramatic courtship and marriage, they gave birth to a son. It's a romantic story that is meant to reflect the hand and heart of God.

Likewise, God has left you a sure, steady path lovingly strewn with goodness. If you faithfully follow these markers, they'll lead you all the way to His heart and home. Your heavenly Father, like Boaz, has taken notice of the impoverished condition of your soul. He desires your well-being, but more important, He desires your companionship. So He leaves a trail for you to follow.

Even before I could identify the giver of these bundles of blessings, I began to collect them and follow on until I met the Holy One. I now recognize these providential markers as holy moments.

Are you ready to discover holy moments in your own life? If your answer is yes, then ask for God's help today!

PERSONAL PRAYER

. . . .

God, You are the creator of heaven and Earth. You have made me in Your own image and created me to fulfill a specific purpose. Please lead me in paths of righteousness for Your name's sake. Orchestrate the minute details of my life for my ultimate good and Your supreme glory. Open up the eyes of my heart to see Your hand at work in all the circumstances that come my way. Please help me to realize that any holy moments I experience are gifts to point me to You, the Holy One. Amen.

CHAPTER TWO

Delight in the Holy One

Take delight in the LORD.
PSALM 37:4, *NLT*

What brings you delight? In *The Sound of Music*, Julie Andrews' character and the Von Trapp children sang a happy tune about a few of their favorite things. Remember? They sang about raindrops on roses and whiskers on kittens, bright copper kettles and warm woolen mittens, brown paper packages tied up with string. . . .

What are your favorite things? You know, the ones that put a smile on your face or a song in your heart? Depending on who you are and what season of life you're in, the source of your delight may vary. For example, toys for tots, machines for men, wardrobes for women, tunes for teens, or recreation for the retired. "Delight" simply describes something that provokes in you a pleasurable emotion, a sense of deep enjoyment or a high degree of satisfaction.

Daily Delights

Daily delights are all around us, if we will only look. We often forget that God will use what we take delight in to accomplish His will. I love to share this story about my husband, Skip, to illustrate this point.

Late one night, before Skip had become a pastor, he heard the pounding surf echoing in his ears and decided to follow Pacific Coast Highway to the Huntington Beach pier. Being a typical Southern Californian beach boy, the salt and sand were a few of his daily delights. As he drove past the oil wells lazily nodding offshore, a sign posted on an apartment window, "Available Now," caught his attention. For some time, Skip had believed that God was calling him to become a pastor. However, he was uncertain of where and how he should minister. Yet at that instant, he remembered something his pastor had said the previous evening: "God is more likely to use people who are available now than those who are waiting for a thunderous voice from heaven to direct them sometime in the future."

While pondering this, Skip parked his car and headed out barefoot onto the empty beach to pray. His destination was one of the many orange lifeguard stations. He scanned the horizon as he climbed the ladder—not another soul in sight. Perched atop the wooden structure with the ocean breeze blowing through his hair, Skip prayed out loud, "Here I am. Send me wherever you'd like. Use me as you see fit. I'm available now!"

Then he waited to hear God's still, small voice.

Instead, his brief prayer was interrupted by a peculiar sound coming from the base of the guardhouse: crunch, crunch, crunch. Skip peered over the edge of his lofty perch, surprised to discover a scruffy-looking boy eating a bag of Cheetos. Skip quickly thought, *Perhaps God wants to use me right here and now*.

"Hey, dude," Skip called out, completely startling the guy noisily munching beneath him. After a few introductory comments, Skip steered their conversation to the One who'd created the roaring ocean. The two beach boys began discussing life and death, sin and salvation. By the end of their conversation, Skip led his fellow surfer in a prayer of salvation.

In the shadow of a moonlit night, just by Skip's being "available now," God had been able to use him. Just by spending time delighting in his favorite place while praying to the Holy One, Skip stumbled quite naturally upon his own holy moment. Humanity and divinity had intersected at a unique point and time, and two lives were changed forever.

As a result, Skip became more convinced that God wanted him to pursue full-time ministry: "That situation taught me that God doesn't merely use those with ability, but availability." Skip encountered God in the midst of one of his daily delights.

Many people assume that an encounter with God can only be experienced through pain and suffering. But there's good news: While trials do teach Christians a great deal, they are not the only catalysts God uses to accomplish His will in our lives. Are you looking for God? If so, He can be found in a valley or on a mountaintop—and in every place in between.

Psalm 37:4 reveals that the Lord speaks as powerfully through pleasure as He does through pain. So, don't make the mistake of only listening for God's voice when disaster hits, or finally reaching out for His hand when there's no place else to turn. Instead, begin to recognize God's still, small voice in the midst of your daily duties and learn to sense His holy presence in places you routinely visit. Like Jacob, you may be journeying along a familiar road, not realizing that "the LORD is in this place, and I was not aware of it" (Gen. 28:16, *NIV*). Or like Elijah, you might be listening for God's voice in a violent windstorm, a tumultuous earthquake or a ferocious fire only to discover it in "a gentle whisper" (1 Kings 19:12, *NIV*).

One of the most important truths of the Christian faith is that we must not only be open to God's surprises, but also ready and eager to embrace them.

True, Lasting Delight

Can lasting joy ever be found in temporal things? God's Word tells us it cannot. Jesus said, "Do not lay up for yourselves treasures on earth, where moth and rust destroy and where thieves break in and steal; but lay up for yourselves treasures in heaven . . ." (Matt. 6:19-20). Things get broken. Possessions lose their luster. Old stuff becomes outdated and has to be replaced with new stuff. When that happens, our things no longer bring us delight; they become a source of disappointment. True, lasting satisfaction is only found in the Eternal One.

When King David said, "Delight yourself in the Lord," I don't think visions of mansions or motorcycles danced in his head. The object of David's delight wasn't a thing; it was the Lord. Learning to delight in the Holy One is the completion of the first step toward experiencing holy moments.

But how do we delight in God?

To show delight in a person, you must discover what brings that person delight. For instance, my list of favorite things includes a thunderstorm sweeping across the desert, curling up with a good book next to a roaring fire, homemade cookies fresh out of the oven, watching old black-and-white movies with a friend. Put them together and I get a little slice of heaven on Earth. This means that if my husband, Skip, decided to plan a day designed to win my affection that included sky-diving before breakfast, rock-climbing after lunch and a four-wheel excursion into the wilderness to roast wild game over an open flame, I would not be thrilled. For Skip to express his love in a way that is meaningful to me, he must get to know me. Once he discovers my delights, the things I like and dislike, he can communicate his love in a way that is pleasing to me.

Likewise, to express your delight in the Lord, you must discover what pleases Him. What does He like or dislike? The Bible uses the word "delight" more than 60 times in reference to the Lord. Most of the instances are associated with obeying

God's laws, following His commands, rejoicing in His testimonies or keeping His statutes. Therefore, to express your delight in the Lord, you must obey His Word. As you do, He will certainly lead you to greater holy moments than you've ever had before.

Another thing that delights God is prayer. Let me tell you the amazing story of some men who delighted in God through prayer and the incredible way God answered their request.

Shortly after Dallas Theological Seminary was established in 1924, its founders were nearly forced to file for bankruptcy. A group of creditors threatened to foreclose at noon on a specific date. Dr. Chafer, the president of the seminary, decided it was best to turn to God in prayer. On the fateful morning the debt was due, he invited several men to his office to intercede with God, who could provide all their needs according to His riches in glory. Dr. Harry Ironside, who later became a well-known Bible commentator and preacher, was also attending that prayer meeting. Harry often quoted the Bible when praying. As was his custom, he petitioned the Lord, "We know that the cattle on a thousand hills are Thine. Please sell some of them and send us the money."

Just outside of the president's office, a tall Texan dressed in western garb, from cowboy boots to a pearl-button shirt, stepped into the business office and said, "I just sold two carloads of cattle in Fort Worth. I've been trying to make a business deal but it fell through. I feel compelled to give the money to the seminary. I don't know if you need it or not, but here's the check!"

The secretary stepped out from behind her wooden desk, took the check from the gentleman and thanked him graciously. Aware of the seriousness of the situation, she decided to interrupt the prayer meeting. Knocking nervously on the door, she entered at Dr. Chafer's invitation. She handed him the check without saying a word, then left unnoticed. Looking at the check, Dr. Chafer was astounded to discover that it was written for the exact amount of the debt! Then he recognized that the endorsement belonged to a cattleman from Fort Worth. Turning to Dr. Ironside, he said, "Harry, God sold the cattle!"[1]

Solomon said, "The prayer of the upright is His delight" (Prov. 15:8). Dr. Chafer and Dr. Ironside understood something every Christian must learn: Prayer and reading the Bible are two of God's favorite things. When they incorporated these godly delights into their lives, God orchestrated an encounter of the divine kind that was unforgettable—a true holy moment.

Answered prayers are holy moments we often fail to recognize. Has God answered any of your prayers? Then you've already experienced a holy moment of your own.

As you make prayer a part of your ordinary routine, don't forget to be on the lookout for God's extraordinary response. The Lord said, through the prophet Isaiah, "It shall come to pass that before they call, I will answer; and while they are still speaking, I will hear" (Isa. 65:24). Answered prayer provides an endearing, reassuring connection between you and your loving Creator. Warren Wiersbe wrote, "Sometimes the Lord encourages you with a very special answer to prayer. It's His way of saying, 'I like what you're doing and what I'm seeing in your life.'"[2]

God's Favorite Things

In addition to prayer and obedience to His Word, God has more favorite things. Here is a brief list I discovered while studying His Word, followed by a short definition and an example of a biblical character that portrayed that attribute. Take time to evaluate whether you currently display these attributes in your daily life.

- ☐ *Fear of the Lord:* "The LORD delights in those who fear him, who put their hope in his unfailing love" (Ps. 147:11, *NIV*). The fear of the Lord is a respect or reverence toward our awesome God, which should prompt us to avoid sin. It's motivated by a love for God that desires never to offend Him, while also striving to please Him in all things. Fearing God is another way of describing holy living or godly behavior. It's produced in our lives through the work of the Holy Spirit, and great blessing is offered to those who display it.

While the children of Israel were captives and slaves under the stern hand of the pharaoh in Egypt, two Hebrew midwives modeled the fear of the Lord. Motivated by reverence toward God, Shiphrah and Puah refused to obey the king's wicked edict, which demanded that every male Hebrew child born be killed at birth. Instead, "the midwives feared God, and did not do as the king of Egypt commanded them, but saved the male children alive" (Exod. 1:17). These courageous women feared the Lord rather than man, displaying godly priorities.

☐ *Truth:* "The Lord . . . delights in men who are truthful" (Prov. 12:22, *NIV*). Truthfulness conveys conformity to facts or reality through unswerving faithfulness to a standard. Truth is a moral and personal attribute of God. Jesus said, "I am the . . . truth" (John 14:6). Paul said that the gospel was "the word of the truth" (Col. 1:5). Therefore, for a Christian, truthfulness is conformity to God's moral standards, belief in Jesus Christ and obedience to the Word of truth.

Paul could be described as unswerving in his faithfulness to God's standard. The unstoppable apostle told the truth whether to kings or countrymen. While on trial before Governor Festus and King Agrippa, Paul said, "I . . . speak the words of truth and reason" (Acts 26:25). Doing so could have resulted in a death sentence. Yet he fulfilled the Great Commission, proclaiming the good news of the gospel and nearly persuading King Agrippa to become a Christian.

☐ *Honesty:* "The LORD . . . delights in honesty" (Prov. 11:1, *NLT*). "Honesty" is used to describe someone who is honorable or truthful, a person with an upright disposition. The one possessing this attribute deals fairly with others. The Greek word for "honesty" can be translated as "purity." It describes someone who makes a stand for that which is pure.

Whether outward circumstances brought triumph or tragedy, Job was an honest man with an upright reputation. In one disastrous day, Satan was allowed to destroy everything Job held dear, from family to fortune. Yet Job did not sin. Job's counselors accused him of transgression, claiming that he was reaping what he had sown. But the Bible records that Job "was blameless and upright" (Job 1:1). Job proclaimed his purity through keeping God's commands: "Let God weigh me in honest scales and he will know that I am blameless" (Job 31:6, *NIV*).

☐ *Integrity:* "The LORD . . . delights in those who have integrity" (Prov. 11:20, *NLT*). The person who shows integrity displays a sincerity of heart, a singleness of purpose or a purity of motive.

The Bible portrays Noah, the builder of the Ark, as a single-minded man of integrity. Among a wicked and perverse generation, Noah and his family were the only ones who were moral in their behavior. Moses wrote, "Noah was a just man, perfect in his generations. Noah walked with God" (Gen. 6:9). Peter, the apostle, also noted that besides obediently building an ark, Noah was a preacher of righteousness (see 2 Peter 2:5).

☐ *Lovingkindness:* "'I am the LORD, exercising lovingkindness . . . in the earth. For in [this] I delight,' says the LORD" (Jer. 9:24). Those full of lovingkindness have a deep desire and zeal for God that is displayed by acts of kindness, love, goodness, mercy, grace and compassion.

Most of Joppa knew that Dorcas had the reputation of being a merciful woman. People said that she was "full of good works and charitable deeds" (Acts 9:36). As a seamstress, she often made garments for the poor and widows of her community. She revealed her lovingkindness not with mere words but in acts of generosity and compassion toward those less fortunate.

☐ *Judgment:* "'I am the LORD, exercising . . . judgment . . . in the earth. For in [this] I delight,' says the LORD" (Jer. 9:24). Judgment is either the process of discerning between good and evil or the act of separating right from wrong based upon the standards of God's law.

God offered Solomon, the newly appointed king, anything he wanted. Yet Solomon did not ask for riches or fame. Instead, he said, "Give to Your servant an understanding heart to judge Your people, that I may discern between good and evil" (1 Kings 3:9). Who can forget how Solomon judged between two women, each of whom claimed the same infant as her own? By telling them to divide the baby in two, he exposed their hearts. As he expected, the real mother rejected his proposal, offering the baby to the surrogate rather than see the child die. Solomon's discernment was divinely inspired.

❑ *Righteousness:* "'I am the LORD, exercising . . . righteousness in the earth. For in [this] I delight,' says the LORD" (Jer. 9:24). Righteousness is based on God's standard, not on a human one. It's motivated by a loyalty to God and is displayed through holy and upright living, according to God's Word. It carries the idea of being right, as well as doing right. Those who possess this attribute will show a straightness of behavior or lifestyle.

Wickedness surrounded Lot, who was a resident of Sodom. It couldn't have been easy to remain righteous with such raunchy living by those around him. The temptation to sin must have been immense. Yet God "delivered righteous Lot, who was oppressed by the filthy conduct of the wicked (for that righteous man, dwelling among them, tormented his righteous soul from day to day by seeing and hearing their lawless deeds)" (2 Pet. 2:7-8). Lot's standard of righteousness was based on the Word of God rather than the words of men.

Before moving ahead, take another minute to meditate on this list of God's delights.

Now answer the following questions: In which of these attributes do you take great delight? If your friends or loved ones were to describe your character, would they choose any of the words from this list? What one attribute least describes you? Think of new ways to integrate these godly characteristics into your life.

We Need to Let Go

My dog, Cleo, has a favorite squeaky toy that has been slobbered on, chewed apart and buried in the backyard. It's her prize possession. If I try to snatch it from her mouth, she runs in the other direction. Even if I walked into the backyard with a T-bone steak to tantalize and entice her to drop the dirty squeaky, Cleo would still rather have that old toy. There's simply no reasoning with my canine companion that her favorite thing is a piece of junk.

But aren't we like that sometimes? Don't we treat our "stuff" as beautiful when, in fact, it's banal? We may strut about proudly, like the Emperor in his new (no) clothes, only to discover that our wardrobe is rather threadbare. What we must do instead is exchange our filthy rags for Christ's robes of righteousness. We must let go of some of our favorite things in order to pursue God's favorite things—His holy delights. And God has an amazing exchange program. Just look at Isaiah's prophecy, in which God promises "to give them beauty for ashes, the oil of joy for mourning, the garment of praise for the spirit of heaviness" (Isa. 61:3).

Do you have any junk you're having difficulty letting go of? One piece of junk I had a hard time letting go of was the need to please. I picked up that powerful compulsion shortly after my parents divorced, during my impressionable elementary school days. That tragedy left me with a sense of responsibility and blame. Perhaps it was my fault that Mom and Dad couldn't stay together. I mistakenly believed that if I did everything just right, then events in our family life would turn out all right.

The day my mother told us of the separation, I set myself on a crusade to fix broken things through my behavior. I took on the role of the consummate middle child—placing myself in between two disenfranchised parties. If only Mom knew how much we loved Dad, she'd take him back. Perhaps I could communicate this to her. If only Dad knew how much we needed Mom, he'd apologize and come home. I reasoned that if I wrote him the perfect letter, got better grades in school or dressed like an angel, this tragedy could be reversed.

When my older sister, Suzanne, cried herself to sleep at nights for months in reaction to the divorce, I shifted roles with her. I became like the big sister, thinking that self-will and determination could make things better. Somehow I must fix it. The truth is, no matter how hard we try, we can't fix people. That is God's business.

Trying to be perfect only created a façade. What was visible on the outside couldn't begin to reveal the emptiness on the inside. By the time I was in college, I had developed two insatiable needs: to feel loved and to be unconditionally accepted by a man. The loss of an everyday father figure left me searching to fill a gaping void. If love couldn't keep my parents together, I believed I would never be capable of loving a man enough to marry one. Since I had no concept of "real love," I settled for counterfeits, moving from one unhealthy relationship to another.

But I didn't stop there. I also tried to fill the black hole in my heart by having a "good time"—which included drinking, smoking pot and developing a vulgar sense of humor. Outwardly, I maintained a 3.5 grade-point average, worked part-time in a swank department store and, with a major in fashion merchandising, I dressed like a model on the cover of

Seventeen magazine. But these "perfect" trappings couldn't contain the turmoil I felt inwardly. So, like many others of my generation, I self-medicated to keep up the veneer. I was a walking contradiction.

Something happened my sophomore year that tore off my mask of perfection, exposing my true self just beneath the surface. My father changed radically from atheist doctor and law student to a born-again Christian and disciple of Christ. One rainy winter day, at Pirate's Cove in Newport Beach, he was baptized by Chuck Smith, the pastor of Calvary Chapel in Costa Mesa, California.

Everything I had embraced in life—including my disbelief in love and my hedonistic lifestyle—was now challenged by Dad's newfound faith. I began to fall into a downward spiral of depression. The years of living a double life were catching up with me—and none of my "medications" was effective enough to stop the light from shining right through my outer shell into the depths of my soul. These burning questions irritated me: "What if Dad is right and I'm wrong?" "What if there is a God?" "What if heaven and hell truly exist?" As I headed for Southern California on summer break, I was determined to check out Calvary Chapel for myself.

Every Sunday morning, Chuck invited people to come forward for prayer, but I was too ashamed to join the many others making their way to the altar. I couldn't escape feeling dirty and unacceptable in the eyes of God. Determined to find the cleansing and closeness I desired with God, I eventually left my seat on a painful journey to the prayer room. As I walked down the aisle, each step caused my burden to increase to an unbearable degree. I thought everyone present could see behind my façade.

Musician-turned-pastor Malcolm Wild greeted me in the prayer room. This gentle man with the honest gaze was a huge fan of Charles Finney, the great nineteenth-century revivalist who helped to bring godly repentance to thousands of people's lives and hearts, and it showed. Malcolm asked me a probing question: "Have you repented of your sins?" At first I was startled. After all, it was a very bold question. Even more, I was unfamiliar with biblical terms and thought repentance meant wearing a large sign that warned "The end of the world is near!" So I told Malcolm, "I have no idea what that is."

He responded, "Repentance means to have a change of heart and direction, to turn from sin and turn toward God. Sin separates us from God but confession brings forgiveness." Then he quoted Isaiah 1:18: "'Let us reason together,' says the LORD, 'Though your sins are like scarlet, they shall be as white as snow.'" And that's when God's compelling truth hit me: I had been too ashamed of my past to accept God's mercy. But this Bible passage declared that God was ready and willing to cleanse anything I might be guilty of!

As Malcolm spoke, my heart began to thaw like an icicle yielding to the sun's warmth. Tears began to run down my face. My fake, "perfect" veneer was melting. When Malcolm asked, "Would you like to pray now for forgiveness?" all I could do was nod in agreement. With voice wavering and hands shaking, I repeated a prayer that set me free from sin and its destructive companion, shame. At long last I was letting go! Absolute relief and a newfound delight swept over me.

After that experience, my feelings of unworthiness never returned. My heart became like a fresh page, and I had a chance to rewrite the story of my life. The Holy One began making me holy as I made His delights my very own. I soon discovered that God reciprocated by delighting in me! The psalmist proclaimed, "He delivered me because He delighted in me" (Ps. 18:19).

The Holiest Moment of All

Have you been holding on to a favorite thing that is, in fact, a filthy secret or dirty old habit? The holiest moment of all awaits you the instant you repent of your sin. Repentance is simply agreeing with God—letting go of what is wrong and reaching out for what is righteous. It's like taking a holy U-turn, where YOU turn from the broad path that leads to destruction to pursue the narrow path whose destination is eternal life. Be assured, "if we confess our sins to him, he is faithful and just to forgive us and to cleanse us from every wrong" (1 John 1:9, NLT). He will gladly exchange your failure for His forgiveness.

The holiest moment you can ever experience is to come face-to-face, heart-to-heart with the Holy One. When you do, you will discover that you are indeed unholy. Only sinners need Saviors. It's only through encountering the Holy One that you can be deemed holy!

Take one of Jesus' disciples, Peter. Peter realized his sinfulness during one of his first holy moments. As a fisherman, he delighted in being out on the Sea of Galilee in his boat. But on one occasion, after spending an entire night at sea, he was disappointed in bringing up only empty nets. In the early morning, as Peter returned to shore, Jesus came to him and instructed him to let down his nets into deeper water. This macho fisherman hesitated, perhaps thinking, *What does a carpenter know about fishing?* Although reluctant, Peter obeyed the Lord's command.

To Peter's amazement, his nets filled so completely with fish that it nearly sank his boat. "When Simon Peter realized what had happened, he fell to his knees before Jesus and said, 'Oh, Lord, please leave me—I'm too much of a sinner to be around you'" (Luke 5:8, *NLT*). Peter's holy moment not only revealed the identity of the Holy One but also the unholiness of his own heart. However, the Lord had plans for that fisherman's future. What was Jesus' reply to Simon Peter? "Don't be afraid! From now on you'll be fishing for people!" (Luke 5:10, *NLT*).

If you haven't experienced the repentance and forgiveness that come from an encounter with the Holy One, why not pray the following prayer? If you choose to do so, you'll discover a delight that far outshines any pleasure this world can offer.

PERSONAL PRAYER

God, please forgive me for pursuing things that delight me but do not please You. Search my heart to expose the sins that separate me from You. Then show me in Your Word what things please You, and help me to pursue them with all my heart. Teach me to make Your delights my very own. Change my heart, O God: replace my fear with faith, my shame with salvation, my despair with holy delight!

Amen.

CHAPTER THREE

Develop Holy Desires

He will give you your heart's desires.
PSALM 37:4, *NLT*

What would you do with a second chance? If you could start your life over or change its direction, what would you do and where would you go? Not long after I surrendered my heart to the Lord, my fresh start began with an inkling of a thought dancing in my mind. Perhaps you could describe this as a desire freshly planted in my heart. You see, never in my life had I experienced such delight and contentment in a pursuit as I had in seeking God. King David said, "Delight yourself also in the LORD, and He shall give you the desires of your heart" (Ps. 37:4). I believe that as I worshiped Jesus, and as I learned His ways and obeyed His commands, He began to cultivate desires in my heart that were His very own!

My budding desire was to become a pastor's wife. What's so amazing is that this newfound desire seemed so natural, almost second nature, as though I'd always wanted to grow up and marry a pastor. My pastor, Chuck Smith, always said, "God moves supernaturally, naturally." In other words, you may not recognize God's hand of providence in the now, but in hindsight His intervention becomes obvious. So, if you'd told me before I asked the Lord to come into my life that I was destined to become a pastor's wife, I would have laughed out loud. But after I was born again, I assumed that every good Christian woman wanted to be a pastor's wife.

One day I told my godly roommate about my little inkling. She looked at me like I was an alien and shouted, "No way! Get thee behind me!" She absolutely couldn't relate. Apparently this desire was unique to my heart. Honestly, I'd never met a pastor's wife and didn't have the faintest idea what one did. Nonetheless, the hunger increased and prevailed until God providentially brought Skip Heitzig into my life. Then my dream came true!

I wish I could say that everything I've ever wished for has been miraculously granted, but I can't. And maybe that's a good thing. Because not everything I've wanted has been a good thing. Like the time I longed to become a buyer for a swank department store. My major in college was fashion merchandising, and I had been voted "best dressed" by my graduating class in high school—I knew how to pull an outfit together and get the designer look for less. But God doesn't focus on outward appearances; He places importance on the heart (see 1 Sam. 16:7).

I've since realized that my desires were shortsighted—God didn't want me to spend my life playing dress-up. Instead, God placed a new desire within me to adorn my heart. Peter wrote, "Do not let your adornment be merely outward; arranging the hair, wearing gold, or putting on fine apparel—rather let it be the hidden person of the heart, with the incorruptible beauty of a gentle and quiet spirit, which is very precious in the sight of God" (1 Pet. 3:3-4).

Oswald Chambers explains that delighting in God puts us in line with His will. When that delight is disturbed, by a hesitation within our spirit or a sense of caution, perhaps it is God redirecting our path. Chambers said, "When you are rightly related to God, it is a life of freedom and liberty and delight; you are God's will and all your commonsense decisions are his will for you unless he checks. You decide things in perfect delightful friendship with God, knowing that if your decisions are wrong he will always check. When he checks, stop at once."[1]

If your dreams have been shattered, perhaps it's for a good reason. God might be trying to direct you on a different path. Maybe He's opening the door to a fresh start that leads to the holy moment of a lifetime!

Your Heart's Desires

What kind of things do you wish for? What are the secret desires of your heart? "Desire" simply means "to wish or want; to crave or long for an object or experience."[2] That sounds innocent enough, doesn't it? What's the harm in wishing upon a star, like Pinocchio did? Or who could blame you for longing for adventures somewhere over the rainbow, as Dorothy longed? Even though the craving of our storybook characters seemed innocuous, their desires lured them into taking dangerous journeys, eventually bringing them the realization that everything they needed was back home.

I've discovered that following the desires found in our unredeemed hearts can take us off course. In fact, God has warned, "The heart is deceitful above all things, and desperately wicked; who can know it? I, the LORD, search the heart, I test the mind, even to give every man according to his ways" (Jer. 17:9-10).

We may not be able to navigate the deep waters of the human heart, but God can. He's shown me how to steer my heart in the right direction. By exposing my desires to three simple questions, What do I want? Why do I want it? What am I willing to do to get it? I can avoid dangerous obstacles and enjoy smooth sailing.

What Do I Want?

The first determination of whether a desire is right or wrong is found in the object of your desire. It depends on what you want. For instance, there's a big difference between looking for love and longing for lust. My mother warned me, "Be careful what you wish for . . . you may just get it." In fact, that is precisely what Samson's mother told her son when he wanted to marry a Philistine, a woman from a race with which the

Jews were strictly forbidden to intermarry. His mom tried to persuade Samson to obey God's commands and choose a bride from among his own people, but to no avail. What Samson desired more than anything was Delilah. And when he got her, she was his undoing (see Judg. 16). Samson should have asked himself, "Do I want what God wants?"

Why Do I Want It?

The second test to discern if your desire is helpful or harmful depends on why you want what you want. Is the desire for greedy gain or God's glory? Motive is a key factor and that's exactly where Eve stumbled. When the serpent asked her, "Has God indeed said, 'You shall not eat of every tree of the garden'?" (Gen. 3:1), Eve passed the test with flying colors, telling the devil that since God said no, she wouldn't even touch the forbidden fruit. So why did Eve ultimately succumb to temptation? Because Satan presented her with an enticing motive: "For God knows that the day you eat of it . . . you *will be like God*" (Gen. 3:5, emphasis added). With this incentive in her heart, "the woman saw that the tree was . . . *desirable to make one wise*, [and] she took of its fruit and ate" (Gen. 3:6, emphasis added). And when she did, it was the downfall of the human race. Eve should have asked herself, "Why do I want what God doesn't want?"

What Am I Willing to Do to Get It?

Finally, the litmus test of a desire's merit lies in how you go about getting it. Many a misguided dreamer has attempted to get the right thing the wrong way. You must ask yourself, "What am I willing to do to get what I want?" In Acts 8, we read about the radical conversion of Simon the sorcerer who had "astonished the people of Samaria, claiming that he was someone great, to whom they all gave heed, from the least to the greatest, saying, 'This man is the great power of God'" (Acts 8:9-10). Simon loved the limelight, but he was outshone by the signs and wonders God performed through Philip. Simon's star was further eclipsed when Peter and John baptized believers with the Holy Spirit. The ex-sorcerer became so envious of their power and prestige that "he offered them money, saying, 'Give me this power also, that anyone on whom I lay hands may receive the Holy Spirit'" (Acts 8:18-19). Peter harshly rebuked him, saying that God's Spirit is not for sale and His servants cannot be manipulated with a bribe. Simon should have asked himself, "What makes me think I can get the right thing the wrong way?"

God-Given Desires

If there's such a thing as wrong desires, then how can we know what are the right desires? What did David mean when he said that God would give us the desires of our heart? The answer is found in the source of these desires—do they originate with our heavenly Father or our fallen nature? God does not grant us every wish or whim—He is not some heavenly genie in a bottle. But He does promise to plant His holy desires within His children's hearts. In other words, as we delight ourselves in

God, He places desires in our hearts that please Him.

In order for desires to be holy, they must be according to His will, His Word and His way. Consider the following Scriptures:

- His Word: "If you abide in Me, and My words abide in you, you will ask what you desire, and it shall be done for you" (John 15:7).
- His will: "We can be confident that he will listen to us whenever we ask him for anything in line with his will" (1 John 5:14, *NLT*).
- His way: "You can ask for anything in my name, and I will do it, because the work of the Son brings glory to the Father" (John 14:13, *NLT*).

Our Perfect Parent

From the time that Nate, our son, could talk, he knew that he wanted weapons. Even before he could speak, he knew how to make the sounds of each and every implement of death. His desire was to amass an armory that rivaled any storybook hero's. At Knott's Berry Farm, he wanted a bullwhip just like Indiana Jones. At Toys-R-Us, he craved a revolver like Dick Tracey's. And in Hawaii, he begged us for a machete like Crocodile Dundee's. When he picked up a huge knife in a tourist shack, we both shouted, "No!" No parent in his or her right mind would let a three-year-old wield a blade of that magnitude. It was quite simple: When Nate asked for something that was not according to our will, we got in the way.

Thank God, when Nate turned 16, his desires changed. Instead of weapons, he wanted wheels. Before he had put a license into his wallet, he was already asking for the keys to a car. He had spent the last five years saving every penny from birthdays and Christmases to buy the car of his dreams. With $3,000 in his bank account, we entered the used car lot. And there, gleaming in the sunlight, was a '93 Volvo 850 for just $3,400. It was fire-engine red and in primo condition. Since our son wanted what we wanted—a safe, reliable car—our answer was a resounding yes! When his request was in line with our will, we paved the way.

It's the same with God. He is not just a good Father; He is the perfect parent. Jesus informed moms and dads,

> You parents—if your children ask for a loaf of bread, do you give them a stone instead? Or if they ask for a fish, do you give them a snake? Of course not! If you sinful people know how to give good gifts to your children, how much more will your heavenly Father give good gifts to those who ask him (Matt. 7:9-11, *NLT*).

The lesson is simple, if you want God to say yes to your heart's desires, then make sure that you are asking for something that He desires. If the Lord has been saying no to some of your prayers, perhaps you are asking Him for the wrong thing.

God has a wish list—the things He wishes you would or

wouldn't desire. As you review the lists below, take time to think about what you would have listed before reading these lists. Which of your longings fit into God's "Do Desire" category, and which of them fall into God's "Don't Desire" category?

GOD'S WISH LIST

Do Desire	Don't Desire
Humility	*Wickedness*
LORD, You have heard the desire of the humble; You will prepare their heart; You will cause Your ear to hear (Ps. 10:17).	The LORD will not allow the righteous soul to famish, but He casts away the desire of the wicked (Prov. 10:3).
Godliness	*Delicacies*
LORD, all my desire is before You; and my sighing is not hidden from You (Ps. 38:9).	Do not desire all his delicacies—for they are deceptive food (Prov. 23:3).
Righteousness	*Evil People*
The fear of the wicked will come upon him, and the desire of the righteous will be granted (Prov. 10:24).	Don't envy evil people; don't desire their company (Prov. 24:1, *NLT*).

Do Desire	Don't Desire

Glorifying
LORD, we love to obey
your laws; our heart's desire
is to glorify your name
(Isa. 26:8, *NLT*).

Spiritual Gifts
Let love be your highest goal,
but also desire the special
abilities the Spirit gives
(1 Cor. 14:1, *NLT*).

God's Word
As newborn babes,
desire the pure milk of
the word, that you may
grow thereby
(1 Pet. 2:2).

Fear
He will fulfill the desire
of those who fear Him
(Ps. 145:19).

Have-Nots
Enjoy what you have
rather than desiring what
you don't have. Just dream-
ing about nice things
is meaningless; it is like
chasing the wind
(Eccles. 6:9, *NLT*).

Unholiness
"But as for those whose
hearts follow the desire
for their detestable things
and their abominations,
I will recompense their
deeds on their own heads,"
says the Lord GOD
(Ezek. 11:21).

Riches
Those who desire to be
rich fall into temptation
and a snare
(1 Tim. 6:9).

Special Delivery

I read an incredible account of a man who desired to do God's will, according to His Word and in His way: Late one evening a professor sat at his desk working on the next day's lectures. He shuffled through the papers and mail placed there by his housekeeper. He began to throw them in the wastebasket when one magazine—not even addressed to him but delivered to his office by mistake—caught his attention. It fell open to an article titled "The Needs of the Congo Mission."

The professor began reading it idly, but then he was consumed by these words: "The need is great here. We have no one to work the northern province of Gabon in the central Congo. And it is my prayer as I write this article that God will lay His hand on one—one on whom, already, the Master's eyes have been cast—that he or she shall be called to this place to help us." The professor closed the magazine and wrote in his diary: "My search is over." He gave himself to go to the Congo.

The professor's name was Albert Schweitzer. That little article, hidden in a periodical intended for someone else, was placed by accident in Schweitzer's mailbox. By chance, his housekeeper put the magazine on the professor's desk. By chance, he noticed the title, which seemed to leap out at him. Dr. Schweitzer became one of the great figures of the twentieth century in a humanitarian work nearly unmatched in human history. Chance? No. Providence.[3]

Dr. Schweitzer proved that he possessed heavenly hopes rather than worldly wishes. By answering the Savior's call to the Congo, he clearly knew three things: 1) what he wanted—to do God's will; 2) why he wanted to do it—to fulfill the Great Commission; 3) what he was willing to do to get it—deny himself and take up his Cross.

For Such a Time as This

One of the best-loved Old Testament examples of being in the right place at the right time and responding in the right way to the circumstances God put before her is found in the story of Esther. When we think about her, we mostly remember that she delivered her people by becoming the Queen of Persia. But did you ever consider that Esther may have thought that her life was insignificant? Orphaned at an early age, Esther's Uncle Mordecai adopted and raised her. Tragically, they were taken captive by a conquering army and made refugees. Because of their deportation to Persia, they were identified as members of a hated minority. And being a woman, Esther was considered little more than property to be disposed of as a man wished. How could God's hand of providence be evidenced in her life?

Divine intervention began for Esther when King Ahasuerus fell in love with her at first sight. His previous wife, Queen Vashti, had been banished from the kingdom. The king's counselors came up with a clever way to find a new queen. They gathered the most beautiful virgins in all the land to take part in a beauty contest, and the winner would take all—including the crown and the king's affection. Through His providence, God made sure that King Ahasuerus's heart would be love-struck by a poor Jewess named Esther. "The king loved Esther more than all the other women, and she obtained grace and favor in his sight more than all the virgins; so he set the royal crown upon her head" (Esther 2:17). However, Esther kept her nationality a secret from the king.

In time, a hateful adversary of the Jews, Haman, planned a holocaust against the Jews. He influenced the king to write a decree that called for the destruction of the entire Jewish race. "The letters were sent by couriers into all the king's provinces, to destroy, to kill, and to annihilate all the Jews, both young and old, little children and women, in one day, on the thirteenth day of the twelfth month" (3:13). The motivating desire in Haman's heart was hate.

Grieved by this terrible turn of events, Mordecai, Esther's uncle, pleaded with Esther to take advantage of her God-given influence. It was time that she revealed her true identity and begged the king for mercy on behalf of her people. Mordecai proposed that God's hand of providence had guided Esther to this very moment and cause. He said, "Yet who knows whether you have come to the kingdom for such a time as this?" (4:14). In other words, "Esther, this is your destiny! It is the reason God has allowed you to be made queen of Persia!"

Terrified, Esther asked that her people fast for three days—and she would do the same. At the end of those three days, she would appear before the king, which was a very dangerous thing to do. There was a law in the land of Persia stating that "any man or woman who goes into the inner court of the king, who has not been called, he has but one law; put all to death, except the one to whom the king holds out the golden scepter, that he may live" (v. 11). Esther knew that if she barged into the throne room uninvited, she could be sentenced to death. But Esther would bend the desires of her heart to reflect God's.

The king had chosen her to be queen on the basis of her beauty; God had chosen her on the basis of her character. And now her character rose to the occasion with heroic resolve. She proclaimed, "If I perish, I perish" (v. 16). Esther's intervention on behalf of her people was nothing less than divinely inspired. As a result, the wicked law was rescinded, and Haman was hung on a gallows that he'd prepared for Mordecai. As for Mordecai, he was promoted to second in command, as the Persian people developed respect for the Jews and their God. And Jewish faith was restored as they celebrated a new feast, Purim, in honor of the Lord's divine deliverance (see Esther 7—9).

A Divine Appointment in a Skybox

Not many people have the opportunity to save a nation or become royalty. But God's divine intervention is just as powerfully displayed in the most ordinary places.

Michele never dreamed of having a holy moment in the midst of changing diapers and doing laundry. Life changed radically the day she became the mother of twins. They were double the blessing but twice the work. On June 16, 1999, before the girls woke up, as Michele sat staring at the newspaper, God entered her consciousness through the door of her heart. She burst into tears and intercessory prayer after reading the headline in the *Fort Worth Star Telegram*: "A Family Shattered: Mother of 3-Day-Old Twins Faces Loss of Husband, Son."[4] Since Michele also had twins, she immediately developed a supernatural bond with the unknown woman who had experienced birth and death simultaneously. She made a covenant with God to pray for her daily.

For days, the newspaper was part of Michele's daily devotions as she searched for more insight on how to pray for Kathy Mogayzel, the bereaved mother. One day she read what the babies looked like and what they had been named:

Joy and sorrow, with few emotions in between, fill the beige house with blue trim where Kathy Mogayzel brought her twin infant sons home . . . the healthy brown-eyed boys who weighed in at just over five pounds each are already distinguishing themselves. Bradley appears to be the fiery one, like his older brother, Zack. And C. J., who takes his name from the middle initials of his father and older brother, is more laid-back, like his father.[5]

Days turned into weeks, and still God burdened Michele's heart with the desire to comfort this widow. But, how? She simply trusted that her prayers would be answered in any way God saw fit. She knew she didn't have to be the one who embraced Kathy, as long as other hands reached out to hold her.

Months later, Kathy Mogayzel left her house for the first time since the tragic accident when a friend invited her to see the Baltimore Orioles play the Texas Rangers. Because the Orioles were the favorite team of Kathy's deceased husband, she agreed to attend. And because Michele's husband, John Wetteland, happened to be the clean-up pitcher for the Rangers, she too would be at the game. And that's when Michele and Kathy had a holy moment. While buying two-for-one hotdogs, these two women ended up in the very same line. Michele struck up a conversation that led to the discovery that they both were mothers of twins. Suddenly Michele realized that *this* was the woman she had been praying for. Immediately she invited Kathy to watch the rest of the game in her private skybox. At the end of the evening, God used Michele to introduce Kathy to her deceased husband's hero, Cal Ripken Jr., who offered to sign her jersey. As they parted, Michele told Kathy, "When you think of this night, remember that there's hope in Christ who will bring joy to your life again."

Later Kathy wrote:

Where do I begin to thank you? Not only did you make one of my biggest dreams come true [meeting

Cal Ripken] you have put a smile back on my face
that I never thought would be there again. . . . You are
the closest thing I've met to an angel . . . I do
believe that God put me in the right place at the right
time and then opened a little window in the clouds.

Holy moments occur when we're in the right place, at the
right time, with a righteous cause. They begin the second that
God's providence intersects our lives, setting in motion a series
of events that sweep us into action. Michele's heart had been
burdened with a righteous cause—prayer for a widow. Then,
through God's providential hand, she and Kathy met at the
right place and at the right time. All things really are possible,
especially when we delight in God and faithfully respond to
the desires He plants deep within our hearts.

Martyn Lloyd-Jones said, "Though you are one of the
teeming millions in this world, and though the world would
have you believe that you do not count and that you are but
a speck in the mass, God says, 'I know you.'"[6] While the pos-
sibility of Kathy and Michele ever meeting was slim to none,
the odds didn't matter: God had arranged a remarkable ren-
dezvous to show a hurting woman that He knew her by name
and saw all her pain.

Providence means that the hand of God is in the glove of
human events. Make no mistake about it. God will have His
way. Though He remains invisible, He is in no way indiffer-
ent. Former president of Rochester Theological Seminary,

Dr. Augustus Hopkins Strong (1836-1921) wrote, "Providence is God's attention focused everywhere."

Make certain that the next time God places a desire within your heart, you follow wherever it leads, whether to the jungles of Africa, the courts of a king or a concession line in a sports stadium. Who knows whether you have come to your place of influence for such a time as this? Your holy moment may be just around the corner.

PERSONAL PRAYER

Lord, I confess that my heart has a way of deceiving me. Sometimes I really don't know what is best for me. But You do. Right now, in this holy moment, I give You my heart. Please make it Your own. Remove from it the lusts that originate in my flesh and fill it with the longings from above. I want to want what You want. When I develop desires that are according to Your Word, Your will and Your way, help me to respond to them in faith and prayer. Use me as You see fit, at just the right time and in just the right place. Amen.

CHAPTER FOUR

Dedicate Your Direction

Commit everything you do to the LORD.
PSALM 37:5, *NLT*

Do you find it difficult to make commitments? Is it even harder to live up to them? After saying yes to something, do second thoughts plague your mind? Or does the dread of starting new projects or setting personal goals immobilize you?

If you answered yes to any of these questions, you're probably suffering from commitment paralysis, which is due, in part, to the power our commitments possess. Truthfully, nothing determines your direction and destiny more than the commitments you make. They'll either define you or they'll undermine you. Commitment holds the key to future success and experiencing holy moments. It is how we dedicate our direction to the Lord.

The fear of saying yes torments countless people—and it prevents them from discovering God's best. In *The Yes Anxiety: Taming the Fear of Commitment*, author Blaine Smith looks closely and compassionately at the struggles Christians have with commitment phobia. He says, "People dislike losing freedom and assuming new obligations; thus, commitment fear is at heart the dread of losing control."[1]

Assuming that you are in control is, at best, an illusion. Think about it, can you prevent a drunk driver from shattering innocent lives? Can you stop cancer from ravaging the body of someone you love? Consider Job, who thought he had it made—a place for everything and everything in its place. In a matter of days, he lost it all: his business, his family, his health and his reputation. It didn't take Job long to realize that there was very little he could control. Although God had proclaimed him the most righteous man in all the earth, he was, after all, merely good—not God. Job cried "uncle" when he admitted, "I know that You [God] can do everything, and that no purpose of Yours can be withheld from You" (Job 42:2). When Job relinquished control, he was able to commit his life to the One who ruled the universe. As a result, Job's future was even better than his past. "Now the LORD blessed the latter days of Job more than his beginning" (Job 42:12).

What Does Commitment Involve?

What about you? Have you committed your life to God? Have you been able to "let go and let God"? Another step to experiencing holy moments is to "commit everything you do to the Lord." It may seem obvious, but examining this passage word by word sheds new light on the topic of commitment: (1) What does God desire? *Commitment!* (2) What is the extent of this commitment? *Everything!* (3) What is the response to this commitment? That *you do* something! (4) Who are you committed to? *The Lord!* As you meditate on each of these words more deeply, you'll discover whether you have completely dedicated your direction to the Lord.

Get Yourself Committed

"Commit" comes from a primitive word that means, "to roll away or cast upon."[2] It's meant to encourage us to let go of anxiety and worry by placing it squarely upon God's capable shoulders. Perhaps that is what Peter was meditating on when he wrote, "Cast [roll away] all your anxiety on him because he cares for you" (1 Pet. 5:7, *NIV*). As God places His desire in your heart, you'll be left making some difficult decisions in response. And that can cause stress. But when you cast your cares upon Him, you become carefree! You don't have to worry about anything because God is able to take care of everything. Committing yourself to God is like a trigger, releasing Him to act on your behalf. In other words, you get out of the way so that He can get in the way—sprinkling your path with holy moments.

Like a coin, commitment is a two-sided proposition. On one side, you use your head, choosing a course of action based upon the best information available. On the flip side is your decision to trust in God, knowing that He will fine-tune your direction as you take the next step. Commitment begins a holy collaboration—you move forward knowing that God will guide you safely to His predetermined destination.

The truth is that God wants you to do His will more than you want to know what His will is. Paul told the Philippians, "It is God who works in you both to will and to do for His good pleasure" (Phil. 2:13). Since that is the case, you can be certain that as you are committed to act upon the desires He's given you, He will point you in the right direction, open doors of opportunity and lead you in the way He wants you to go. So get going!

This reminds me of a story my friend Penny told me. One day, as her family was leaving church, her preschool-aged daughter, Erin, ran ahead to open the huge glass door. She pushed and shoved until she was blue in the face. Then she backed up and made a running start at the obstacle. As she hit the door with full force, it opened like the rock wall of the cave when Ali Baba shouted "Open sesame!"

It was comical to watch Erin preen over her seeming prowess. But she was clueless to the fact that her father had slipped his strong hand just above her head, acting as the unseen force that opened the door. It's comforting to think that God does the same for you and me in so many different ways if we'll just get ourselves committed.

Does "Everything" Mean Every Thing?

Exactly how far does God expect us to take this commitment thing? Does it include our circumstances, our careers, our kids, our cars and our clothing? Yes! When God says "everything," He really does mean every thing! The apostle Paul said that in addition to committing everything to God, we must also pray about everything: "Don't worry about anything; instead, pray about everything. Tell God what you need, and thank him for all he has done" (Phil. 4:6, *NLT*). That means it's okay to pray about everything from painful injuries and marriage difficulties to work projects and financial needs. God is interested in the minutest details of your life. He also knows the exact number of your days (see Ps. 39:4-5). Details are His thing! Nothing in your list of everything will overwhelm God. He is equal to the task—and He wants it all.

In her book *The Hiding Place*, Corrie ten Boom tells about an incident that taught her to pray about everything. She and her sister Betsy had been placed in a Nazi concentration camp for harboring Jews in their parents' home. The barracks were extremely crowded and infested with fleas. One morning as they read in their tattered Bible from 1 Thessalonians, they were reminded of God's hand in all things. We'll pick up the story there:

> Betsy said, "Corrie, we've got to give thanks for this barracks and even for these fleas."
>
> Corrie replied, "No way am I going to thank God for fleas." But Betsy was persuasive, and they did thank God even for the fleas.
>
> During the months that followed, they found that their barracks was left relatively free, and they could do

Bible study, talk openly, and even pray in the barracks. It was their only place of refuge. Several months later they learned that the reason the guards never entered their barracks was because of those blasted fleas.[3]

Can you believe that an infestation of fleas is proof that God can use anything and everything to answer the prayers of His children?

Just Do It!

So what are you waiting for? The admonition is to commit everything you do to the Lord. That implies that the Lord expects you to do something. For some of us, the biggest obstacle to success is ourselves—by our hesitation, procrastination or lack of motivation. My dad always said, "Don't put off until tomorrow what you can do today." Don't let an environment of excuses hold you back another day. And don't let the comments of critics slow you down. If you do what you can, God will do what you can't!

This was Englishman William Carey's attitude. His goals could not be curtailed by critics. When he was determined to become a missionary to India, his father attempted to quench William's quest by pointing out his lack of academic qualifications. Why, William didn't even know the language! To that, Carey proclaimed, "I can plod!" God accomplishes mighty things for His kingdom through those who are willing to plod faithfully in the power of the Spirit.[4]

Your Whole World in His Hands

You can breathe a sigh of relief knowing that the commitment you make is "to the Lord" of heaven and Earth. His hands are capable of bearing your whole world, and this great big universe as well. God told Isaiah the prophet, "I am the one who made the earth and created people to live on it. With my hands I stretched out the heavens. All the millions of stars are at my command" (Isa. 45:12, *NLT*). Rest assured, He won't let you fall (see Ps. 121:3), He won't let you fail (see Rom. 8:28), and He won't forget His promises to you (see Isa. 49:15).

With such great assurances, won't you commit your "everything" into His mighty hands today? William Cowper's hymn "God Moves in a Mysterious Way" reminds God's people of how God won't let His people fall or fail. Perhaps you've been comforted by this hymn, but you may not know the amazing story about how God's hand of providence led to its composition.

Even though William Cowper was a Christian, he fell into a dark season of despair. One foggy night, he ordered his coachman to take him to the London Bridge. Suffering from depression, he planned to commit suicide by jumping into the Thames River. However, his coachman got lost and drove aimlessly for hours. Disgusted by the delay, Cowper left the carriage and decided to walk to the London Bridge himself. After traveling a short distance on foot, he discovered that he was at his own doorstep! The carriage had been going in circles. Immediately he recognized that God's providential hand had been guiding his way. Convicted by the Spirit, he realized that the way out of his troubles was to look to God, not jump into the river. As he cast his burden on the Savior, his heart was comforted. With renewed hope he wrote these reassuring words:

> God moves in a mysterious way
> His wonders to perform;
> He plants his footsteps in the sea,
> And rides upon the storm.
> Ye fearful saints, fresh courage take;
> The clouds ye so much dread
> Are big with mercy, and shall break
> In blessings on your head.[5]

Cowper's experience teaches us to be thankful for the cloudy days as well as those that are full of sunshine. God can use a fog bank or a father's advice to accomplish His will. We must continually commit everything, including our lives and our future, into God's hands. When we do, we are dedicating our direction to the course God has preordained for our lives. Let me tell you about a time when I committed my everything to the Lord.

Timely Advice in the Word

Youth With A Mission (YWAM) whammed me with a huge dose of reality when I attended a discipleship training school in Hawaii. For six months, as I put into practice what I was learning, I listened to pimps and prostitutes bemoan their destiny, handed out tracts to tourists, shared my testimony with defiant youths at a detention center and worked at a Christian coffee house on Hotel Street in the notorious red-light district of Waikiki. I soon realized that this school was not for the faint of heart. The amazing thing was that I loved it!

Before heading home to Southern California, Dave and Debbie Gustaveson, the DTS (discipleship training school) administrators, asked me to reenlist as school secretary for the upcoming year. This was not a paid position. In fact, I needed to raise $200 per month for expenses. As I looked at my bank account, I realized that I had just enough money to cover airfare and a month's support. This commitment was an enormous leap of faith. But I believed that "God will meet all [my] needs according to his glorious riches in Christ Jesus" (Phil. 4:19, *NIV*). My pastor's motto was, "Where God guides, God provides." I believed that if God was in it, then money was no problem! After prayer, I told Dave, "I'll serve for the next year."

Back in sunny California, storm clouds of doubt threatened to erode my resolve. I wondered, *What should I do? I don't have the resources to pay for an entire year. Should I wait until I earn all the money needed and then join the staff? Or do I just offer what I have and hope for provision in the future?* I spent a lot of prayer time considering this amazing opportunity and my meager resources. One morning, sitting down with my Bible on my lap, I asked God for His advice.

All at once, the Scripture reference 2 Corinthians 8:10 popped into my mind. Immediately, I opened my Bible to see what the passage said. This is what I read.

> *And here is my advice* about what is best for you in this matter: Last year you were the first not only to give but also to have the desire to do so. Now finish the work, so that your eager willingness to do it may be matched by your completion of it, according to your means. For if the willingness is there, the gift is acceptable according to what one has, not according to what he does not have (2 Cor. 8:10-12, *NIV,* emphasis added).

I knew positively that God had spoken and I must obey. So I ran upstairs to tell my family about God's timely advice.

My dad was not delighted. When I proclaimed, "I'm going back to YWAM to serve as school secretary," he asked, "How much do they pay?"

I mumbled, "Um, it's a nonpaying position. But I'll do it as unto the Lord."

Then he inquired, "And how much does it cost?"

I hung my head, "I—I need to raise $200 per month."

Then he put his foot down. "Lenya, I don't think this is such a good idea. The Bible says to 'honor thy father and mother.' You do not have my approval on this."

I was baffled. God was telling me one thing and my spiritual authority was contradicting it. Who should I obey? I made a beeline for the phone to hear what Dave and Debbie had to say about this. Besides, I had already given them my word. After I explained to them the clarity of God's Word and my father's emphatic veto, their reply was, "Submit to your earthly father and trust your heavenly Father to work it out." Devastated, I resolved to heed their counsel.

Before Dad opened the newspaper that night, I pulled him aside. Assuring him of my love and respect for him, I explained that this was a rare situation in which I was convinced that God had spoken. I showed him the miraculous Scripture passage along with my notes written in the margin, then said, "Nevertheless, not my will but thine be done."

For several days, Dad said nothing. But one morning at breakfast he confided, "Lenya, I've been thinking about what you said. For the last few nights I haven't slept well. I don't want to get in God's way. I'd regret it if some day in the future you doubted God's voice because I stopped you from obeying it today. If you're convinced the Lord's calling you back to YWAM, you have my blessing. But this is your venture of faith. I'll support you prayerfully but not financially."

I returned to Hawaii and served alongside Dave and Debbie for the next year. At the halfway point, my dad had a change of heart and began sending monthly financial support. God provided in His time and in His way. And I learned an invaluable lesson on "committing my way to the Lord."

When I offer Him my future, He takes care of the present. Also, when I'm obedient to do His will His way, He can do anything!

Have you ever read a Bible passage that suddenly stands out as vividly as one red evening gown in a sea of little black dresses? "The word of God is living and powerful, and sharper than any two-edged sword, piercing even to the division of soul and spirit, and of joints and marrow, and is a discerner of the thoughts and intents of the heart" (Heb. 4:12). In other words, God's Word is very *now* and relevant in your current circumstances. If you're looking for timely advice, check your Bible first.

In his book *On Being a Servant of God,* Warren Wiersbe explains the way God uses His Word to direct our paths. He shares,

> Okay, you've waited on the Lord, prayed, and coun-seled with people you trust and to whom you are accountable, and you've decided that God wants you to make a change. But before you write the letter of resignation, wait on the Lord for some word from His Word. No, you don't open your Bible at random and point to some verse. I'm talking about a special word from God in the course of your regular daily Bible reading. Or it may come in the course of regular wor-ship. You'll know that God is speaking to you because the Holy Spirit will make some Scripture vivid and real to you in a way that simply can't be ignored.[6]

Dedicate Your Direction

I use an acronym of the word "commit" to remember what the Bible means when it says "commit everything you do to the Lord." If we follow this reminder, we can be assured that our direction is dedicated to the Lord.

Cast your worries upon the Lord
Offer your future into His hands
Make sure you pray about everything
Map out plans that are scriptural
Identify a course of action
Take the next logical step

As you take that next step, God will begin to make sure that you follow the direction He has chosen for your life. Sometimes He guides by opening a door; other times He will direct your path by closing a door.

Open Doors

Sometimes God leads through opened doors. Father Abraham was old and set in his ways. He wanted Isaac, his son, to marry under one condition: Isaac's bride must be of God's choosing, from among Abraham's family. However, Abraham's relatives lived far away. So he decided to send his most faithful servant, Eliezer of Damascus, on a long journey to find a fiancée for

Isaac. As Eliezer approached his desired destination, he realized the difficulty of determining the identity of Abraham's relatives. While sitting beside the city well, he devised a plan and offered up a silent prayer. He requested that the Lord reveal the right woman through a test: Eliezer would ask the young women coming to draw water to give him a drink. The one who volunteered to draw water from the well for him *and* his camels would be the one (see Gen. 24:11-14).

Before Eliezer had even finished his nonverbal communication with God, the first woman to arrive at the well offered to do exactly what Eliezer had proposed. Of course, she was Rebekah, the daughter of Abraham's brother. Eliezer broke out into praise, saying, "Blessed be the LORD God of my master Abraham, who has not forsaken His mercy and His truth toward my master. As for me, being on the way, the LORD led me to the house of my master's brethren" (Gen. 24:27).

Eliezer's dedication to the Lord is a great example for us to follow. So let's consider his plan of action. First, Eliezer committed everything to God in prayer. Then he made plans based on his present circumstances. Next he got busy and talked to the first woman God brought to the well. Lo and behold, God opened the door to Rebekah's heart! Eliezer realized that "being on the way, the LORD led me." If he had stayed at home or sat on that rock interceding until midnight, or waited for a bolt of lightning from heaven, the door may never have opened. But the moment Eliezer stepped out in faith, God arranged the most amazing answer to his request.

Rick Warren's book *The Purpose Driven Life* reminds us to "work out" our salvation with fear and trembling, and then watch God "work in" our lives according to His good pleasure. Warren wrote, "Obedience unlocks God's power. God waits for you to act first. Don't wait to feel powerful or confidence. Move ahead in your weakness, doing the right thing in spite of your fears and feelings. . . . You don't just sit around and wait for it to happen."[7] Sometimes it takes a huge leap of faith to commit your life into the hands of God.

Closed Doors

Sometimes God leads His people by closing doors. The apostle Paul was a go-getter. If it were possible, he'd be one step ahead of the Lord. There were times that God had to slow down this overly ambitious man. Once, as Paul was on a whirlwind tour through the region of Galatia, heading straight toward Asia, God slammed the door shut. He was "forbidden by the Holy Spirit to preach the word in Asia" (Acts 16:6). But that didn't stop Paul. If he couldn't go east, then he'd head due north. "But the Spirit did not permit them. So passing by Mysia, they came down to Troas" (Acts 16:7-8). He'd already come from the south. God wouldn't allow him to go north or east. The only direction left was west. That night Paul had a vision: "A man of Macedonia stood and pleaded with him, saying, 'Come over to Macedonia and help us'" (Acts 16:9). Paul got the message. By discovering where not to go, he was pointed into the direction he should go. Paul heard a few nos from God before he got a yes.

Don't be discouraged if you bump into roadblocks. God can lead just as miraculously through a no as He can though a yes. I once heard Ruth Graham say, "I would have married the wrong man if God had said 'yes' to all of my prayers."

What About Those Roadblocks?

To her friends, Debbie Lascelles was known as "the Texas cream puff." She knew all the current makeup techniques, could style her hair into the perfect "Texas 'do" and could paint her nails to match any outfit. But there were some things Debbie couldn't do, like change a flat tire. She had adopted this philosophy of life: "Don't learn to do something you don't want to end up doing." For instance, never ask your husband to teach you how to use the lawnmower unless someday you expect to be trimming the grass. I've been told that Debbie wouldn't even screw a new license plate onto her car. Instead, she asked an able-bodied maintenance man working on staff with her at the YWAM base in Tyler, Texas, to do the job for her.

She was at the top of her class when she graduated from nursing school and was voted the most likely to succeed. Everybody knew that Debbie was destined for a prosperous career and would probably marry a doctor. But God interrupted her plans by calling her to the mission field, despite her previous protests. At 35, she and three other like-minded Christians joined Voice of the Martyrs (VOM) on a missions trip to the Sudan. They were to bring much-needed supplies—

clothes, medicine and books—to a remote village in the middle of the steamy jungle. The team was also asked to teach their native brothers how to win their enemies to Jesus.

It was a sweltering hot day as they loaded the supply truck, and the Texas cream puff felt like she was melting. She poured herself into the seat next to another missionary dripping with sweat and fastened her seatbelt for the bumpy ride ahead. They knew they must travel all day to make their destination before nightfall.

Halfway through the trip a tire blew, and their hearts deflated too. The only way to change the tire in that heavy-laden truck was to empty its contents. When the team finally overcame the obstacles of unloading the truck and changing the tire, too much time had been lost. They would never reach the village before dark. Disappointed, they decided to turn back.

Suddenly there was a rumbling out of the afternoon sky. Their escorts feared the worst, saying, "Those are enemy bombers! Everyone hit the dirt." Debbie the debutante was now sweaty, dirty and scared. But to her amazement, the planes roared by without noticing the team or the truck. Like heat-seeking missiles, the bombers remained locked on their target—the very village where Debbie and her team had been headed. The time of detonation? Just before dark. A flat tire saved their lives.

Making the long, grueling trek, only to be disappointed when she could not reach her destination became a holy moment for Debbie. God had said no and placed His loving hand as a roadblock in her path.

Has God ever answered one of your prayers with a deafening no? Take time to reflect on the reasons why. Perhaps He was protecting you from a bad decision or attempting to lead you to greener pastures. If that's the case, you've had a holy moment. Look for supernatural surprises in unexpected places—not only when God leads you through an open door, but also when He closes it.

PERSONAL PRAYER

*Lord, I admit that I am afraid of making commitments.
It's hard for me to surrender control into Your hands.
But I know that's foolish. You're the only One capable
of leading me in the way everlasting. Give me the courage
to let go and let You take control of it all. Today, I'm offering
You my everything: everything I have, everything I am,
everything I hope to be. Lord, give me the wisdom to make
plans pleasing to You, and afterwards to step out in
boldness of faith. Open and close doors before me as
You see fit. Lead me to Your desired destinations.
Amen.*

CHAPTER FIVE

Depend Wholly on Him

Trust him.

PSALM 37:5, *NLT*

"Love means never having to say you're sorry," was perhaps the most histrionic (and most quoted) line delivered in any movie during the 1970s. Another overly sentimental phenomenon from that era was a comic strip called "Love is . . ." It featured a cupidesque couple extolling the virtues of love with silly captions like, "Love is . . . carving your initials on a tree." Or "Love is . . . being kinda 'corny.'" And my personal favorite was, "Love is . . . remembering to replace the toothpaste cap."

We know that love is a desirable commodity—everyone loves to be in love. But what defines love? Certainly not the "Love is . . ." definitions. And sometimes you do have to say you're sorry more times than is comfortable! I would suggest that the most important component of true love is that you trust the one you love. You can have confidence in who the person is and what the person says and does.

I decided to do an experiment by having my friends tell me what they think trust is. I asked several people whom I trust these questions: How would you define the word "trust"? When you think of someone who is trustworthy, what qualities or characteristics does he or she possess? Can you list other words used interchangeably with the word "trust"?

With these inquiries in mind, I challenged them to complete the following sentence: "Trust is . . ." Their answers were insightful:

Trust is . . . being confident that what someone else says is true. —Terri Shinn

Trust is . . . being totally vulnerable with another person. —Dick DeBeck

Trust is . . . the confident expectation of promises fulfilled. —Skip Heitzig

Trust is . . . earned. —Penny Pierce Rose

Trust . . . believes that someone is as concerned about you and your safety as you are. —Suzanne Friesner

While one friend was attempting to define trust, her teen-aged daughter, Kylee, who was eavesdropping in the background, interrupted. She blurted out, "Trust is faith!"

"That's it!" I exclaimed. "Biblically, 'faith' and 'trust' are synonymous. These concepts are inextricably intertwined." Throughout the Bible, in the overwhelming majority of cases, "faith" means "trust" in God. In the Gospels, when Jesus spoke of faith, all except one time the apparent sense of the word was "trust." The same is true of the apostolic writings. In them, with rare exceptions, the word "trust" precisely fits the context as an alternative to "faith."[1]

Kylee's profound insight made me wonder how great men of faith had defined trust. Their answers were enlightening.

"Trust involves letting go and knowing God will catch you."[2] —James Dobson

"Trustfulness is based on confidence in God, whose ways I do not understand. If I did, there would be no need for trust."[3] —Oswald Chambers

"Faith is not belief without proof, but trust without reservation."[4] —Elton Trueblood

"Faith is a refusal to panic."[5] —Martyn Lloyd-Jones

"Faith is not believing that God can, but that God will!"[6] —Abraham Lincoln

Now it's your turn. Take a moment to complete the sentence, "Trust is . . ." Articulating your definition of trust is vital. Why? Because it reveals the depth of your faith by exposing the foundations upon which it is built.

Psalm 37:5 exhorts believers to trust in God. The Old Testament idea of trust conveys much more than confidence, hope or surety in another. It was often used in reference to a city that was secure from attack or impending danger. The cities of Israel could dwell in security from imminent doom or potential danger because God offered to keep them safe, if they trusted solely in Him to protect them. The promise of security was contingent on the nation's faithfulness to and trust in God. This same guarantee is available to all who put their trust in the Messiah.[7] Therefore, when David exhorted believers to "Commit your way to the LORD; trust in him," he was implying an unswerving faith in an unstoppable God.

The Five *W*s of Trusting God

To gain greater insight into understanding the kind of trust to which the psalmist referred, we'll explore the five *W*s (the *who, what, when, where* and *why*) of trusting God. Throughout the rest of this chapter, we'll examine the answers to these questions: *Who* do I trust? *Why* can I trust Him? *When* should I trust Him? *What* strengthens my trust in God? *Where* can I trust Him more? As you consider these questions, you'll be able to mentally gauge your trust quotient and see where you might be failing to trust in the Lord.

Who Do I Trust?

The object of your trust is crucial because it has the potential to make your faith flourish or flounder. My friend Holly had an encounter with a suspicious sojourner while on a trip to the Middle East that taught her a great deal about the object of a person's trust and how fickle our feelings can be. During an excruciating 11-hour flight to Israel, Holly was assigned to seat 15A. Walking down the aisle, came a man with the physique of Arnold Schwarzenegger, hair shorn into a Neo-Nazi "skinhead" style, clothing riddled with rips and all exposed flesh graffitied with tattoos. As he approached Holly's row, she silently prayed, "O dear Lord, please don't let him sit in 15B!" When he collapsed into the empty seat beside her, the rest of the church group headed for the Holy Land collectively gasped.

After stilted introductions, Holly's new travel companion, Jake, rolled up his sleeves for dinner, unveiling a tattoo on his left forearm like the crescent moon and star of Islam. To break the ice, Holly asked, "I see you have a Hubal. Are you a Muslim?"

Although Jake had insight into the teachings of Muhammed, he confessed he was not Islamic. "I admire Allah and the way his followers are dedicated to purity and prayer. That's why I got the tattoo."

While Jake was holding out his coffee cup to the flight attendant for refills, Holly saw another tattoo on Jake's right arm—this one resembled a saint. By now, Holly's curiosity was piqued. She was compelled to ask, "Is that a saint? Are you Catholic?"

Jake answered, "Nah, my second tattoo of the Elephant Buddha—which was supposed to protect me and give me good luck—made me really sick. Turned out I got hepatitis from a dirty needle."

An incredulous Holly interrupted him, saying, "I'm sure that was a big red flag. You stopped getting tattoos after that, didn't you?

"No way!" Jake said, "I did my research. Turned out that Catholics experience miracles by praying to saints. That's why

I have St. Luke, the patron saint of doctors on my bicep."

In an act of sheer exhibitionism, Jake removed his T-shirt, exposing a large tattoo etched between his waxed shoulder blades. "This here's the Chinese yin and yang symbol." He went on to explain: "Yin is Chinese for moon, and yang means sun. The Chinese watch the seasons for balance. This yin and yang shows I accept life's cycles."

As the captain dimmed the cabin lights, Jake pulled out a bottle containing a colorful collection of pills. After washing down a couple of sleeping tablets with water, but before falling into drug-induced slumber, Jake shared how each tattoo represented what he considered to be the best that each religion had to offer. His tattoos gave him a feeling of serenity.

Holly asked Jake about the obvious contradictions inherent in the different philosophies represented on his body. She tried to point out the glaring inadequacies of these Eastern religions and philosophies. But Jake refused to listen. He was content to swallow the attractive nuggets of truth just as easily as he swallowed his pills. He never saw the competing worldviews the various religions offered, nor did he have the discernment to sift away the deceptive chaff that encased them.

Jake was a perfect illustration of what trust is *not*. He attempted to glean the good from each religious ideology, without maintaining loyalty to any particular one. Jake seemed unaware that the definition of God from these respective religions was mutually exclusive. If one religion that you embrace defines God as personal and all knowing, how can you trust the God of another religion who is impersonal and finite? Jake was a walking paradox.

The Bible makes it clear that it's impossible to trust Jesus, Muhammed and Buddha simultaneously. Allegiance to one means disloyalty to the other. Jesus said, "No one can serve two masters; for either he will hate the one and love the other, or he will be loyal to the one and despise the other" (Matt. 6:24).

As you reflect on Jesus' words, ask yourself who you trust in the most—in people or in God? On a scale of 1 to 10, with 10 indicating that you have total trust in God, what number would you say indicates where your trust is right now?

Your trust in God is strengthened as you get to know Him in a deeper and more personal way. In other words, to know Him is to trust Him. David proclaimed, "Those who know your name trust in you, for you, O LORD, have never abandoned anyone who searches for you" (Ps. 9:10, *NLT*).

How does knowing God's name engender trust? In the culture of the Old Testament, a name meant a great deal. For the Hebrew people, a person's name represented his or her character. In Scripture, we frequently see someone give a new name or title to God after experiencing His presence up close and personal. To know God by name requires a personal experience with Him. Each of God's names possesses a meaning and a message.

Names are important because they provide a form of self-revelation. For instance, some know me as Lenya Heitzig.

But those who know me more intimately call me Lenya May. It's a term of endearment and familiarity. So, if you call me by my first and middle name, you reveal that you have a personal relationship with me. It means you know that I'm feisty like my Granny May Farley and creative like my Aunt Lotte Lenya. And only my husband calls me Ladybug, a nickname he adopted early in our courtship.

Likewise, the different names for God reveal different attributes of His character. As you get to know God on more intimate terms, you're invited to call Him by some of His special names—you get to know Him on a first name basis, if you will. When you are weak, He is El Shaddai—the Almighty God (see Gen. 28:3). Should your bank account dwindle, He is Jehovah Jireh—the Lord who provides (see Gen. 22:14). If you are lost and afraid, He is the Good Shepherd of your soul (see Ps. 23:1). During seasons of doubt and confusion, He is the Wonderful Counselor (see Isa. 9:6). When wars rage without, He is the Prince of Peace within. When you develop a deep relationship with Him based upon who He is, you will trust Him more and more.

As you reflect on God's attributes, does that knowledge affect how much you trust Him? Would you say that up to this point, you have been trusting in others more than in God?

Why Can I Trust Him?

I propose that we can trust the God of the Bible because He is trustworthy. He's earned our trust through His promises and

His faithful fulfillment of them. We can place our firm belief in God because He keeps His promises in a way that is consistent with His other character traits, such as His honesty, His truthfulness and His justice. All that I have seen God do teaches me to trust Him for all I have not yet seen.

The psalmist extolled God's reliability in the Old Testament: "As for God, his way is perfect. All the LORD's promises prove true" (Ps. 18:30, *NLT*). Paul confirmed in the New Testament that God is the ultimate promise keeper: "For no matter how many promises God has made, they are 'Yes' in Christ" (2 Cor. 1:20, *NIV*).

How often do we act upon the promises God has given in His Word? Franklin Graham once shared a very daring concept with me called the "God room." The idea is to live in such a way that we give God room to be bigger than life. He told me that we should attempt something so great for God that it's doomed to failure unless God comes through on our behalf.

Franklin learned the "God room" principle from Bob Pierce, founder of Samaritan's Purse. Pierce once told Franklin: "'God room' is when you see a need and it's bigger than your human abilities to meet it. But you accept the challenge. You trust God to bring in the finances and the materials to meet that need. You get together with your staff, prayer partners and supporters, and you pray. But after all is said and done, you can only raise the resources required. Then you begin to watch God work. Before you know it, the need is met. At the same time, you understand that you didn't do it. God did it. You allowed Him room to work.'"

Franklin asked, "Does this always work? I'm not sure I've got that kind of faith."

Pierce smiled back and said, " 'God room' is when you've seen a need you believe God wants you to meet. You try to meet it, but you can't. After you've exhausted all your human effort, there's still a gap. . . . That's when you pray, leaving room for God to work."[8]

Do you give God room to be God in your life? If you do, you'll be more likely to experience a holy moment. What comes to mind when you think of what God has done on your behalf?

Let me tell you the true story about a young woman who was willing to trust God while dangling 100 feet in the air. Brenda, an adventurous student, decided that learning to rock climb was the perfect way to overcome her fear of heights. One summer day, she joined a group of enthusiasts on a daring ascent up a solid rock face. At the halfway point, while affixed to her instructors' carabiner, Brenda reached a precarious ledge where she stopped for a breather. Accidentally, the instructor at the top of the precipice snapped the rope, which hit against Brenda's eye and knocked her contact lens loose.

If you wear contact lenses, as I do, you know how impossible it is to find a lens once it is out of sight. While suspended 100 feet above ground, and with blurry vision, Brenda asked God to help her find the wayward contact lens. She hoped it was lodged somewhere under her eyelid. After groping slowly upward to the summit, she had a friend examine her eye with a flashlight. No lens.

Glancing out across the mountain range, Brenda thought of the verse: "For the eyes of the Lord run to and fro throughout the whole earth, to show Himself strong on behalf of those whose heart is loyal to Him" (2 Chron. 16:9). She proclaimed, "Lord, You see all these mountains. You know every single stone and leaf on them. You know exactly where that lens is." As Brenda's team made their way back down the trail, a new party of rock climbers was ascending. One shouted ahead, "Hey, anybody up there lose a contact lens?" Overjoyed, Brenda yelled back, "It's mine! I lost it midair." When they reached one another, Brenda asked how her fellow climber had found the stray lens. He said that while looking down, he was shocked to discover an ant moving slowly across the face of a rock carrying a contact lens!

Brenda's dad is a cartoonist. When she told him about her holy moment, he drew a comic strip with an ant lugging a huge contact lens on its back. The caption read, "Lord, I don't know why You want me to carry this thing. I can't eat it and it's awfully heavy. But if this is what You want me to do, I'll carry it for You."[9]

For Brenda, trusting God despite difficult circumstances was a wonderful opportunity for a caring God to build a fearful girl's faith. She gave God room to hear her prayers, keep His promises and fulfill His Word. Brenda understood something that every Christian must grasp: Trust is not a feeling, it is a choice firmly based upon God's ability, credibility and availability. A decision to trust the Lord may be accompanied by good feelings. But genuine trust is best displayed when we rely on Him in spite of our negative feelings. Holy moments happen more frequently to those who trust the Holy One in spite of emergencies or emotions.

When the going gets tough, do you make decisions based on your feelings or on God's faithfulness?

When Do I Trust God?
The psalmist wrote, "O my people, trust in him *at all times*. Pour out your heart to him, for God is our refuge" (Ps. 62:8, *NLT*, emphasis added). Some people believe that trust is just for the big stuff, like when a doctor says, "It's incurable!" Or the banker says, "It's overdrawn!" Or your spouse says, "It's over!" However, failing to trust God with the small stuff is where I often stumble. My problem lies in holding false assumptions. I mistakenly think that I can handle the little things as long as God takes care of the big problems. But that's not trust at all. Trust is for the big stuff, the small stuff and all the stuff in between!

Trusting God, a profound book written by Jerry Bridges, offers this insight:

> [A] pitfall in trusting God, which we are prone to fall into, is to turn to God in trust in greater crisis experiences of life while seeking to work through the minor difficulties ourselves. A disposition to trust in our-

selves is part of our sinful nature. It sometimes takes a major crisis, or at least a moderate one, to turn us toward the Lord. A mark of Christian maturity is to continually trust the Lord in the minutiae of daily life. If we learn to trust God in the minor adversities, we will be better prepared to trust him in the major ones.[10]

My friend, Dianne, told me the following story. It illustrates perfectly the concept of trusting God at all times.

A wealthy employer, who possessed an estate on the ocean, a yacht docked at the shore and multiple foreign cars parked in the garage, invited an employee and his wife to dinner at one of the finest restaurants in town. Because they couldn't afford this kind of extravagance, they were intrigued and a bit intimidated.

As the three entered the exclusive eatery, the boss stopped suddenly, stared down at the pavement and then stooped over to pick up a penny lying on the street next to a cigarette butt. He held it up in his manicured hand and with a smile placed it in his pocket as though it were a pearl of great price.

How absurd, the employee's wife thought to herself. *This man needs a penny like he needs another pebble for his handsomely landscaped yard. Why bother picking it up?* Throughout dinner, the strange scene plagued her. She casually mentioned that her daughter once had a coin collection and asked the wealthy man whether the penny he had found was valuable.

Grinning like Alice in Wonderland's Cheshire cat, he removed the penny from his pocket and held it out in front of her.

"Look at it," he said. "Read what it says."

She read aloud, "United States of America."

"Not that; what else?" he challenged.

"One cent?" She questioned.

"No, keep reading."

Impatiently she said, "What? In God We Trust?"

The well-appointed gentleman nodded, saying, "If I trust in God, then I believe that His name is holy, even on a coin. Every single coin minted in the United States has that reminder stamped on it. But most of us never seem to notice. It's as if God drops a message right in front of us to trust Him. Who am I to pass it by? So, when I find a stray penny, I stop to ask myself whether my trust *is* in God at that moment. Picking up that penny instead of passing it by is my way of telling God that I do trust in Him. I think it's God's way of starting a conversation with me. Lucky for me, God is patient and pennies are plentiful!"[11]

How about you? Do you trust God with the daily minutiae as well as the major dilemmas in your life? Philip Bennett Power, Scottish minister and author, wrote:

The daily circumstance of life will afford us opportunities enough for glorifying God in trust, without our waiting for extraordinary calls upon our faith. Let us remember that the extraordinary circumstances of life are but few; that much of life may slip past without their occurrence; and that if we be not faithful and trusting in that which is little, we are not likely to be in that which is great. . . . Let our trust be reared in the humble nursery of our own daily experience, with its ever recurring little wants, and trials, and sorrows; and then, when need be, it will come forth, to do such great things as are required of it.[12]

As you reflect on the passage above, ask yourself, When do I trust God—rarely, sometimes, or always and in all ways?

What Strengthens My Trust in God?

Solomon wrote, "Trust in the LORD with all your heart; do not depend on your own understanding. Seek his will in all you do, and he will direct your paths" (Prov. 3:6, *NLT*). I wish I could say that I've always trusted the Lord. But the truth is, I've often failed the test of trust. And when I don't trust God, it's often due to conflicting emotions—or because I think I know better than God does.

A few years ago a situation arose that clearly illustrates that conflict. Sadly, my own intuition competed with God's divine inspiration. Looking back, I can see how He tried to direct my path but I didn't follow His lead.

This situation took place on a typical day for a pastor's wife and mother. I had dropped Nathan off at Georgia O'Keefe elementary school and stopped to pick up dry cleaning on the way to the gym. After going for a long run with my friends, I showered in the locker room and dressed for the day. Following a lunch appointment with a hurting church member, but before picking up Nathan from school, I had an hour of free time. As I drove down the street, I thought, *Lord, what do You want me to do today? Is there anything you'd like me to be available for? What should I do with this time?*

With these questions running through my mind, I noticed that I was driving past Manor Care, an assisted living center. I remembered that Pete Sowa, a kind, disabled war veteran, was hospitalized there. Suffering from a severe stroke, he required full-time nursing assistance. On the previous Christmas, we had visited Pete the ex-pilot and were thrilled to hear him retell his World War II stories. My reverie was interrupted with a notion, a sense from the Lord that I should pay Pete an unexpected visit. Wouldn't it be nice to simply remind Pete that I loved him?

But before I pulled into the parking lot, another thought competed with the first. Perhaps I should run home and balance the checkbook. And then I remembered the mountain of laundry on my closet floor. Within moments, I veered my car out of the turn lane and back into the flow of traffic that led home. I rationalized that I could always visit Pete another day.

The next morning, as I cleared the breakfast dishes, the phone rang. Mary Sowa, Pete's faithful wife, called to say hi. *What a coincidence*, I thought. *I'll ask her when it's a good time to visit*

Pete. But before I could, Mary interrupted, "Lenya, Pete died last night in his sleep. He's gone home to be with the Lord." I gasped, and my eyes filled with tears. I felt deep grief. The Lord had given me the opportunity to say good-bye to Pete, and I had missed it. I had balanced my checkbook but not my priorities. To this day, my heart longs for that last good-bye.

I missed a holy moment. But it taught me an important lesson. Not every thought I have originates with me. Sometimes God plants an idea within my mind that leads to a holy moment, if I'll only trust and obey. Now if I have a flash of inspiration, I'm more likely to act on it.

Has God has been nudging you to make a timely phone call, give a generous donation or take decisive action? There is no time like the present! As you respond to His initiative, you won't miss the holy moment that may be waiting just for you.

Where Can I Trust Him More?

It's easy to believe in providence when it's working to our advantage. But if things get shaky, we mistakenly think God has fallen asleep at the wheel. Charles West said, "We turn to God when our foundations are shaking, only to learn that it is God who is shaking them."[13] Providence can be a double-edged sword. Remember Queen Esther? In order for Esther to be in, Queen Vashti had to go out. In the moment, God's providence can appear harmful, but it will become helpful after future realities come into view. God promises His children that all things will always turn out for the best in eternity.

Paul said, "We know that all things work together for good to those who love God" (Rom. 8:28). Only time will tell the whole story of God's providential care in your life and in the lives of others.

The life of Joseph perfectly illustrates this concept. When Joseph was betrayed by his brothers and sold into slavery, it seemed that the hand of providence was against him. But slavery led Joseph to Egypt where he was made second in command to Pharaoh. Through Joseph's interpretation of a prophetic dream and his wise counsel, Egypt was sustained through a terrible famine. Years after his brothers' betrayal, Joseph told them, "You meant evil against me; but God meant it for good, in order to bring it about as it is this day, to save many people alive" (Gen. 50:20).

Perhaps, like Joseph, you're experiencing a season of being misunderstood, falsely accused or imprisoned unjustly. Don't give up! This situation is exactly where you can trust Him more. Allow God to work all things together for your good and His glory as you wait patiently for His deliverance. A bad thing can become a good thing if it leads you to something better! When you're in a situation that you don't quite understand, ask yourself, In what area is my trust challenged?

Making the Leap

The more we depend on God, the more dependable we find Him to be. Understanding *who* He is—Almighty God; *why* He is trustworthy—because He keeps His Word; *when* He can be trusted—with the little and the large stuff; *what* strengthens our trust—intuitions or His inspiration; and *where* we can trust Him more—wherever He leads; equips us to experience more holy moments. The question is, Do you trust in the Lord? If not, please offer this simple prayer to the One who is completely trustworthy.

PERSONAL PRAYER

Jesus, I call upon Your matchless name, asking for the strength to trust You without wavering. I know that there are situations where I have relied on my emotions or intuition instead of on Your promises. Please help me follow Your gentle leading. I don't want the details of my life to distract me from even one divine opportunity. Here's my heart, Lord, tune it to trust You, and turn it to obey You both now and forever. Amen.

CHAPTER SIX

Destined for Divine Encounters

And he will help you.
PSALM 37:5, *NLT*

Imagine having X-ray vision like Superman. You could see past obstacles and through walls. At parties, you could mesmerize guests as you revealed the contents of their unopened purses and wallets. Finding the elusive belt hiding somewhere in the bowels of your suitcase wouldn't be a problem either. What an incredible asset X-ray vision would be!

Superman not only possessed X-ray vision, but he also was blessed with telescopic vision, enabling him to span the solar system in a glance. As well, he had microscopic vision, allowing him to see the tiniest dust particle. But there were two things Superman could not see: anything encased in or hidden behind a wall of lead, and future events.

God has it all—X-ray vision, telescopic vision, microscopic vision and future vision. He declares, "I am God, and there is no other; I am God, and there is none like me. I make known the end from the beginning, from ancient times, what is still to come. I say: My purpose will stand and I will do all that I please" (Isa. 46:9-10, *NIV*). Nothing, not even kryptonite, can prevent Him from accomplishing His will.

Biblical scholars define God's future vision as providence. The word "providence" comes from the combination of two Latin words: *pro,* meaning "before," and *video,* meaning "I see." It literally means "foresight." *Merriam-Webster's* defines "providence" as "divine guidance or care; God conceived as the power sustaining and guiding human destiny.[1] Not one detail of your life takes Him by surprise. He sees what you do and why you do it. The motives within the human heart are penetrated by God's watchful eye. "The LORD does not see as man sees; for man looks at the outward appearance, but the LORD looks at the heart" (1 Sam. 16:7).

Through His providence, God not only orchestrates details in the lives of individuals, but also that of entire nations. One of America's Founding Fathers, Benjamin Franklin, said, "The longer I live, the more convincing proofs I see of this truth, that God governs in the affairs of man; and if a sparrow cannot fall to the ground without his notice, is it probable that an empire can rise without his aid?" You might say that history is "His story"!

Kings, presidents and military officers unwittingly fulfill God's plan as agents of providence. For instance, around the time of Jesus' birth, Caesar Augustus needed more money for his war campaigns. Like most politicians, he thought that raising taxes was a good way to get it. So he legislated a tax initiative mandating that all citizens be registered in the city of their birth (see Luke 2:1,3). If you were looking over Caesar's shoulder, you may have thought, *Hmmm. That's incredible. This decree could fulfill a prophecy given nearly 700 years ago by Micah, making sure that the Messiah is born in Bethlehem* (see Micah 5:2). The census tax forced Mary and Joseph to travel to their hometown, Bethlehem, while Mary was great with child. Was Caesar a powerful ruler? Perhaps. Was he a pawn in God's plan? Absolutely!

How can we, as finite human beings, grasp the immensity of God's purview and knowledge? Perhaps a simple analogy will help. Have you ever stood on the sidelines and watched a parade, such as the famous Rose Bowl Parade in Pasadena, California, go by? You have to wait to see each float, each marching band, each equestrian unit. But if you watched the televised parade, you could get some aerial shots from the Goodyear Blimp that floats over the parade and see the beginning to the end, and everything in between.

Let's pretend that you and I go to the Rose Bowl Parade in Pasadena, California. We arrive the night before and camp out on Colorado Boulevard right in the middle of the parade route between Orange Grove and Sierra Madre Boulevards. The next morning we're thrilled when our favorite float, depicting a winter wonderland glides past. Next comes the marching band we've been waiting for—The Canadian Massed Pipes and Drums—dressed in their mixed Scottish tartans playing traditional music on their bagpipes and drums. Just then, some late-comers push their way to the front. Breathlessly, the lady asks, "Did I miss the Rose Queen? She's my second cousin. We were delayed by traffic."

We assure her that she's made it in time. In fact, if she walks back a few blocks, toward Orange Grove Boulevard, she'll be able to see what is yet to come—she can view the future before it becomes our present.

Her husband interrupts, "But did we miss The Canadian Massed Pipes and Drums? I'm Scottish."

We're sorry to tell him, "Yes, but if you run ahead, to-ward Sierra Madre Boulevard, you can see what has already transpired."

At that moment, my cell phone rings. It's my mother, in Michigan, calling to say that she's watching the whole thing on her television. They just showed an aerial view of the parade from the Good Year blimp. She has seen the end, the beginning and everything in between. She tells us, "Don't miss the equestrian unit of miniature horses. They're adorable."

As you can see from our parade passing by, perspective is everything. Depending on your vantage point along the parade route, you can see the past, the present or the future of this wondrous spectacle.

In a limited sense, the aerial view is how the timeline of his-tory appears to God. He has a bird's-eye view of the events tak-ing place on planet Earth. He can observe all aspects of time simultaneously. Therefore, He is able to act providentially in our lives. He knows what's going to happen before it happens; and He knows how the past can intersect the present.

Let me tell you about one of those times when God knew what was coming before one of His children did.

Tomorrow's Too Late

Have you ever heard of Dr. Helen Roseveare, the famous British missionary doctor to the Belgian Congo (now Democratic Republic of Congo)? Her life's motto was, "If Christ be God and died for me, then no sacrifice can be too great for me to make for Him." As a single woman, she served for 20 years overseas while enduring incredible hardship. At one point she was taken captive by rebel soldiers. During the five months of her captivity, she was brutally beaten and raped. But Helen knew that her relationship with God had not been damaged. In fact, God redeemed those horrible events by making her a counselor to female missionaries who have been abused. Now in her 80s, Dr. Roseveare continues to serve the Lord. She travels tirelessly as an internationally acclaimed spokeswoman for Christian missions, mobilizing people by showing them that God uses imperfect people with real struggles to be His ambassadors to the world.

She tells about a holy moment that displayed God's incredible hand of providence in the lives of some young orphans. One evening, she attended a young mother giving birth to a premature baby girl. Despite Dr. Roseveare's best efforts, the mother died, leaving the tiny infant and a crying two-year-old daughter. Dr. Roseveare knew that without an incubator or electricity, it would be difficult to keep the baby alive because of the cold, drafty nights. She asked a native assistant to fetch the hot water bottle to keep the infant warm. However, they discovered that the hot water bottle had burst. Dr. Roseveare instructed the nurse to hold the child as close to an open fire as safety would allow to help the child survive the cold night.

The following day, Helen gathered the other orphans for prayer time. She told them about the newly born baby, the two-year-old orphan and the broken hot water bottle. Ruth, a precocious 10-year-old, prayed, "Please God, send us a hot water bottle. Tomorrow will be too late, God, because the baby will be dead by then, so please send it this afternoon." The staff was shocked by the prayer's boldness. Yet Ruth continued, "While You're at it, would You please send a doll for the little girl, so that she knows that You really love her?"

Helen said she knew in theory that God was capable of doing anything—the Bible said so. But she had her doubts. Besides, she hadn't received any parcels from England for nearly four years. Also, who back home would think that they needed a hot water bottle in tropical Africa?

Later in the afternoon, while making her rounds, Dr. Roseveare heard a car drive down the dirt road. When she returned to her apartment, she was astounded to discover a large parcel on the veranda. As tears welled in her eyes, she called the orphans so that they could open the box together.

In addition to clothes, bandages and snacks, a new rubber hot water bottle was in the box! Ruth, who was sitting in the first row, shouted, "If God sent the hot water bottle, He must have sent the doll too!" Then she dug to the bottom of the parcel and pulled out a beautiful little doll. She insisted that they take the doll to the little two-year-old girl so that she would know that Jesus loves her.

The parcel had been on the way for five months, sent by a women's Bible study group. One inspired woman had been so obedient to God that she even sent a hot water bottle to the equator. And one of the ladies had given a doll, 5 months before a 10-year-old African girl would pray, "We need it this afternoon, God." The words Jesus said are true: "Your Father knows the things you have need of before you ask Him" (Matt. 6:8). God saw what was needed before the prayer was uttered. Through His divine providence, He was able to arrange the details of the past to benefit a situation that would take place in the future. His fingerprints were all over that parcel!

He Will Bring It to Pass

Providence best describes the final phrase in Psalm 37:5: "He shall bring it to pass." This is the last simple step to discovering God's fingerprints in your life. Be confident, knowing that if you've taken the biblical steps we've spoken of—delighting in Him, developing holy desires, committing everything you do to the Lord, and trusting God with everything—He will surely do His part of bringing about that which concerns you.

While most commentators agree on the meaning of "He shall bring it to pass," some of their remarks impart a fine distinction to explain its intent. I've listed some of their different interpretations to help you grasp this key phrase better:

—He will work.[2]

—He will secure a happy result.[3]

—He will take care of your interests.[4]

—He will accomplish what you desire to be done, but cannot do yourself.[5]

—Leave the guidance of thy life entirely to Him; He will gloriously accomplish all that concerns thee.[6]

This final step may be the hardest for you to accept, because there's nothing left for you to do. Now it's time for you to simply wait, and watch God move, looking for His handiwork in your life. As Moses exhorted the children of Israel just before the Exodus, it's time to "stand still, and see the salvation of the LORD, which He will accomplish for you today" (Exod. 14:13).

Moses and the people had done all that God had asked them to do. They obediently celebrated the Passover by sacrificing the Lamb, sprinkling blood on their doorposts, and preparing unleavened bread. After the Angel of death had killed the Egyptians' firstborn, the Israelites asked for back wages in the form of precious metals. Then they departed in haste into the wilderness to meet with God. But the hardhearted Pharaoh changed his mind. He ordered his army, including 500 chariots, to chase and subdue the renegade nation.

With the army behind them, desolate wilderness flanking them on the left and on the right, they faced a dead-end at the Red Sea. There was nowhere to run and no place to hide. It was humanly impossible to escape. So Moses reminded the people to let go and let God intervene on their behalf, trusting that "He will bring it to pass." As an act of faith, Moses simply stretched forth the rod in his hand and then witnessed God's salvation.

How about you? Has God been asking you to make a symbolic gesture of faith? Perhaps He's asked you to fast and pray. Maybe He's told you to keep quiet and believe. Or you know that you must stop trying to accomplish God's will in the power of your own might. There's nothing you can do to change the situation or make things better. That is the perfect place for God to work. Jesus said, "The things which are impossible with men are possible with God" (Luke 18:27). Today could be the day that you simply raise your arms in surrender.

Moved by the Hand of God

Sacrifice and surrender are just what the Methodists of Swan Quarter, North Carolina, did in the fall of 1876. They had decided to build a new church for the glory of God on a highland spot right in the center of town. After selecting this perfect location, the congregation was distraught when the land's owner, Sam Sadler, refused to sell them his property. They raised more money and offered Sadler a higher price. But hard-hearted Sam would not make the deal. Undaunted, the citizens built the new church on a low-lying piece of property out on Oyster Creek Road toward the edge of town. On September 16, 1876, they cheerfully dedicated to the Lord their small white-framed building sitting on brick pilings.

Weather historian Merlin S. Berry shares what happened next.

That same day a major hurricane was churning past Cuba on its way toward the Carolina coast. As the hurricane spun across the state, winds drove high waters across Pamlico Sound and piled them on the shores of Hyde County. Three days later, much of Swan Quarter was flooded with five feet of water. Homes and businesses were deluged and wrecked, and the town's fishing fleet was severely damaged.[7]

Despite the devastation all around them, the residents of Swan Quarter were awed by an act of divine providence: The powerful hurricane had hoisted the small church, intact, right off its foundations; it then gently floated on a direct route to the exact piece of property on which the congregants had originally intended to erect their building. Everyone was in awe of God's intervention. Sadler was so overcome that he later signed a deed donating his land to the Methodist church. Today, a sign stands in front of the Providence Church, reminding visitors that this was the church "Moved by the Hand of God."[8]

By now, you may be wondering, *How do I know where the hand of God is leading me?* It has been suggested that you can compare discovering God's will with a sea captain's docking procedure.

A certain harbor in Italy can be reached only by sailing up a narrow channel between dangerous rocks and shoals. Over the years, many ships have been wrecked, and navigation is hazardous. To guide the ships safely into port, three lights have been mounted on three huge poles in the harbor. When the three lights are perfectly lined up and seen as one, the ship can safely proceed up the narrow channel. If the pilot sees two or three lights, he knows he's off course and in danger.

God has also provided three beacons to guide us. The same rules of navigation apply—the three lights must be lined up before it is safe for us to proceed. The three harbor lights of guidance are (1) the Word of God (objective standard), (2) the Holy Spirit (subjective witness) and (3) circumstances (divine providence). Together they assure us that the directions we've received are from God and will lead us safely along His way.[9]

God still leads us and devises incredible outcomes from ordinary beginnings. What seems uneventful to us today may be the preparation for something colossal. That's the way it happened for me one pristine fall afternoon in Albuquerque, New Mexico.

Mercy B.A.N.D.s

I can still hear my car radio playing praise music in the background. I had just hung up my cell phone from talking with my mother. Her words, "God has given you so many holy moments that you could string them together like pearls on a necklace," echoed in my thoughts.

Something bigger than me began forming in my mind. After the horror of 9/11, I had continually cried out to God, "What can I do? How can I help the hurting?" I was painfully aware that I was not a rescue worker digging through the rubble in the aftermath of terror. I was not a soldier putting my life on the line in a fight for freedom. I was just a housewife, living hundreds of miles away from New York City, in the town where the Rocky Mountains come to an end. I was desperate for someone, anyone, to tell me how to respond to this tragedy in a personal way, as Americans did when they donated scrap metal to aid the war efforts during World War II.

Imperceptibly, my thoughts shifted from resignation to realization: *It's impossible to wrap my brain around the loss of nearly 3,000 lives. But it's possible to wrap my heart around one victim.* I realized that one-to-one was the key!

That's when God breathed an idea pregnant with potential into my heart: What if sterling silver bracelets were engraved with the names of each 9/11 victim? And what if individuals across the United States wore these bracelets as a daily reminder to pray for God to heal the hurting? Similar to P.O.W. bracelets of the late '60s and early '70s, these wristbands would offer a personal connection to tremendous loss and pain. The bracelet would eventually be named "Mercy B.A.N.D."—an acronym for "Bearing Another's Name Daily." Further, these little silver linings could serve as a living memorial to those who died tragically, as a daily reminder to pray for their loved ones, as a symbol of hope in God's mercy to heal our wounds, and as a promise of blessing to those who are merciful.

What an epiphany! But I recognized there was a major league problem—*me*! I'm not an entrepreneur who knows how to launch a timely idea. The how-tos overwhelmed me. Looking for an easy way out, I called someone capable of completing this project—Franklin Graham of Samaritan's Purse International. Franklin loved the notion. But he challenged me, saying, "Do it yourself and watch God move." That's when a series of holy moments appeared in my life, like precious pearls formed in a sea of pain.

The first pearl emerged during a "chance meeting" one Saturday night in October. Jan, who worked at the church, informed me that her husband (whom I'd never met) was a jeweler. That night at church, for the first time, I notice Jan walk down the aisle with Norm, her husband, at her side. I shot out of my seat like a human cannon ball to introduce myself and tell Norm about Mercy B.A.N.D. "I'll do anything I can, Lenya," he said. "The bracelets aren't hard to make. But I'm not an engraver." Cocking his head, Norm added, "But hey, there's this guy named Phil Scott. If you can track him down, he's an engraver." As if on cue, Phil entered the sanctuary. Norm enthused, "That's him! That's Phil Scott!" After animated introductions, Phil enthusiastically joined the Mercy B.A.N.D. team.

Some may think, *What's so holy about that moment?* But how do you explain the miraculous meeting of three strangers in a church building the size of a soccer field, with more than 12,000 attendees and 4 services from which to choose? I believe that only God can orchestrate a holy moment in which three lives intersect at the right place, at the right time, with the right skills to get a job done for His glory!

The second pearl surfaced the next morning through a "timely" phone call. Unable to sleep after such an exciting night, my mind was reeling with ideas and questions: How much should the bracelets cost? What about shipping and postage? Where would I put the inventory? I pondered the names of several businessmen as possible candidates to give me counsel. I decided Vic Jury was the one I'd call first.

As I reached for the phone, its ring startled me. Norm was on the line, "Hi, Lenya, Phil and I met this morning. It will take over a year to produce 3,000 bracelets with just two guys hammering them out in a garage. But an engraving machine might cut the time in half."

While pondering the price of an engraving machine, I explained that we could divide the fee for the machine into the cost of each bracelet in order to defray the debt. Norm interrupted my seemingly perfect logic, saying, "Lenya, engravers run close to $10,000—I have a catalog right in front of me."

I don't know how it slipped out, but I heard myself say, "I have faith. I know God will provide. Look what He's done already." I'd never felt that kind of faith well up within me before. Norm seemed encouraged by my faith, but he wasn't willing to put himself into financial jeopardy based upon my beliefs.

I decided now was a good time to call Vic for advice. I explained the vision for Mercy B.A.N.D., recounted the providential meeting with Norm and Phil, listed the costs and ended with the need for an engraving machine. Vic chuckled, then replied, "Lenya, I have an engraving machine. It's tucked away in an empty room in my warehouse. It's available for this project any time, night or day." Within 20 minutes of my first phone call of the morning, I was able to call Norm and announce, "You'll never believe what God did! We have an engraving machine and a warehouse."

Unbelievers may explain these holy moments as mere chance or a fluke. But too many coincidences were piling up to think it was luck. I was convinced that God had purposely left handfuls of "wheat" on my path as a token of His love—just as Boaz had left wheat in the grain fields of Bethlehem for Ruth to glean.

The next morning, the third pearl in a string of holy moments dropped into my lap. I got up to do what I do every Monday morning—go to the gym for a workout. While lifting weights with my friend Karen, I recounted the supernatural events God had orchestrated. Karen, a non-Christian, blurted: "You're giving me goose bumps! The hair on my arms is standing straight up!" I finished my too-good-to-be-true story with this lament, "Six months is too long. I don't know how to make the bracelets faster." Suddenly Karen stood still. "Lenya, the woman who works out after us owns a manufacturing company that makes sterling silver jewelry for QVC, the home shopping network. Her name's Carol Felley. Give her a call!"

After a quick shower, I called Felley Manufacturing and set up an appointment for later that afternoon. At the meeting, Carol and her brother Ira explained that they were Jewish transplants from New York City and were looking for a way to help their hometown. They were overjoyed to offer their expertise to Mercy B.A.N.D.

While choosing the weight of sterling silver, the width of each bracelet and the font for engraving, I fielded a call on my cell phone: Roger Flessing of the Billy Graham Evangelistic Association (B.G.E.A.) wanted to let me know that his organization would plug the Mercy B.A.N.D. with an article in *Decision Magazine* as well as air an interview on the "Decision Today" radio program. Now the bracelets would be endorsed by the most trusted organization in the Christian world!

Then Roger asked, "How many bracelets are you ordering?" Unsure, I said, "I'm thinking either 300 or 3,000." He said, "Think bigger! You should multiply your largest estimation by 10 or 20."

My knees began to tremble as tears came to my eyes. I thought, *That means nearly 20 people would be honoring every person who died on September 11, and praying for the survivors! God, Your ways are not my ways. Just as You said in Ephesians 3:20, You are doing "exceedingly abundantly above all that we could ask or think." Thank You for Your blessings.*

Gamblers might assume I was on a roll. But I knew that divine intervention was stacking the odds in my favor. Solomon said, "We may throw the dice, but the LORD determines how they fall" (Prov. 16:33, *NLT*). With God's hand in this venture, I knew I couldn't lose.

Pearls started popping up everywhere and with such frequency that within two days, Bob Church, the administrator for Calvary of Albuquerque, had found donors for office space, a telephone system, computers, shelving—as well as a contractor who would get the office wired for business. Brochures with instructions on how to pray the Lord's Prayer were donated free of charge. By Sunday, just eight days after my first encounter with Norm, the first set of bracelets, gift boxes and brochures arrived in our newly equipped office space. We were ready to distribute our first Mercy B.A.N.D.s.

But the next pearl was buried in the midst of confusion. Thursday morning, Bob called with some sobering words of caution: "Lenya, I've been thinking about Mercy B.A.N.D. What if it's not legal to put the names of deceased people on a bracelet without permission? Let's take a step back and consult an attorney."

Hanging up, I cried out, "Lord, how can this be wrong? Why would You bring me this far only to close the door now? Show me what to do." In a daze, I walked downstairs muttering, "A lawyer. Who do I know that's a lawyer?"

As I made lunch, I was interrupted by a ringing telephone. My friend Steve, an international businessman from North Carolina, said, "I was driving down the freeway when you came to mind. So I called to see if everything is okay." After a few niceties, it dawned on me that Steve was an attorney. I shouted in his ear, "Steve, you're a lawyer!" In a torrent of words, I told him about Mercy B.A.N.D. By the end of the day Steve found an intellectual copyright attorney to make sure that everything was legal. And the cost for the legal advice? It was free!

The biggest Doubting Thomas would have to admit that this phone call was not serendipity or synchronicity. It was a supernatural surprise planned by the Savior. God often works supernaturally naturally. In the moment, a situation may seem mundane. But in the future, while looking back at that situation, you become acutely aware that it was indeed miraculous.

I would love to tell you about the 20 volunteers who worked nonstop, scouring newspaper articles and Internet sites to uncover every person lost that fatal day, weeping and praying as they typed each name into our database. I wish you could have volunteered in the call center where family members began calling to request a bracelet bearing their loved one's name. I'll never forget meeting Becky, the wife of Alfred

Marchand, whose name I bear on my bracelet. Alfred was a retired police officer turned flight attendant who explained his career change saying, "Someday if an airplane goes down, I want to be there to tell the other passengers about Jesus."

Then the holy moments came fast and furious: Astoundingly, during the anthrax scare, we were able to have 100 Mercy B.A.N.D.s hand-delivered to every senator on Capitol Hill. Several newspapers from the *Washington Times* to the *Dallas Morning News,* and countless television and radio programs from across the nation covered the Mercy B.A.N.D., exposing millions of people to the project and to God's mercy. I was humbled when *Nightline* in New York City aired an interview with me in November 2001. Unbelievably, a simple housewife in Albuquerque, New Mexico, who prayed, *Lord, what can I do to help the hurting?* found herself on national television telling the nation, "God is full of mercy and compassion."

In less than a year, over 60,000 Mercy B.A.N.D.s were distributed coast to coast and to foreign countries. Nearly 2,000 bracelets were given, at no cost, to family members, thanks to a generous donation.

But most precious to me is a scrapbook I've kept full of cards, letters, photos and memorabilia that family members have sent to Mercy B.A.N.D., thanking us. I still cry when I read what they wrote. I wish to share some of their thoughts with you so that you can see how God's holy moments can transform our ordinary lives—yours and mine—if we continually look for God's leading and then respond!

- What has been consistently helpful to me, as well as my family, has been the kindness extended by others. Your thoughtfulness in providing the Mercy B.A.N.D.s will be a gentle reminder of how precious life is. I hope as others wear their bands they reflect on the goodness in this world and how that goodness will overcome evil.—Jacque Van Laere Hayes, whose brother Daniel perished at the World Trade Center

- I wanted you to know that you have touched my heart, and I appreciate all of your prayers. . . . My wife, Shelley, is a hero, and you can be proud to wear her name on your wrist.—Don Marshall, husband of Shelley, who died at the Pentagon

- Thank you for honoring the victims of September 11 with Mercy B.A.N.D. It is ironic that I have a POW bracelet from the Vietnam War and one from the Persian Gulf War that I bought to remember the victims. I never dreamed that one day my daughter's name would be on a band as a victim of war, a war that we didn't even know we were in.—Nancy May, mother of Renee, crew member aboard American Airlines Flight #77

- Today in the mail we received the Mercy B.A.N.D.s for my sons Peter and Tommy Langone. Just wanted to thank you for them and for conceiving of the idea; they are very well done. So many people have been so kind and generous in their support and we do appreciate it.—Sheila Langone, mother of Peter of the FDNY and Tommy of the NYPD

I'm convinced that these bracelets were a symbol of God's love to the hurting relatives of the 9/11 tragedies. For some unfathomable reason, He used ordinary folks to be His ambassadors of compassion. As students, secretaries, retired senior citizens and senators wore Mercy B.A.N.D.s and offered silent prayers, they showered the victims with God's abundant mercy and grace.

Holy moments don't occur only in times of national tragedy; they also happen in the midst of everyday life. Oswald Chambers, author of *My Utmost for His Highest*, said: "The disciple who is in the condition of abiding in Jesus is in the will of God, and his apparent free choices are God's foreordained decrees. Mysterious? Logically absurd? But a glorious truth to a saint."[10]

God's fingerprints are frequently hidden on the surface of ordinary events and are equally visible to all Christians who are willing to identify the impressions He's left. I've never uncovered such an incredible dusting of holy moments before, and probably I never will again. However, this experience has reminded me of the importance of recognizing them when they do happen and thanking God for making such a great impression in my life.

Seeing His Hand in Your Life

Do you long to have holy moments as much as I do? I wouldn't be at all surprised if you've already experienced many such moments but simply failed to recognize them. Perhaps what you thought was a chance meeting, a timely phone call, a coincidence or luck was actually evidence of God's providence—a holy moment.

Start looking for God's hand at work in your life. Reflect on the five fingerprints found in Psalm 37:4-5, and you'll become more keenly aware of holy moments when they do occur. Remember, *delight* in the Holy One; *develop* holy desires; *dedicate* your direction; *depend* wholly on Him; *discover* holy moments. As you do, your eyes will behold God moving mysteriously. He will intervene with holy moments tailor-made to suit you. And you'll also realize that the Holy One is nearer to you than you imagined. He surrounds you with His presence. Paul reminds us, "He is not far from each one of us; for in Him we live and move and have our being" (Acts 17:27-28).

The Lord longs for your companionship. Remember that holy moments are meant to draw you closer to the Holy One. They are God's way of tapping you on the shoulder or whispering sweetly in your ear. Please don't disregard His overtures of affection. Be sure that you acknowledge Him with praise, prayer and a passionate pursuit for deeper intimacy with Him.

My prayer is that you will be amazed to discover the deep impression that holy moments make in your life. May you be able to trace their origin from your yesterdays all the way forward to your tomorrows, where untold instances of God's goodness and grace await.

PERSONAL PRAYER

Lord, I want to see Your hand of providence in the everyday circumstances of my life. Open my eyes to see how You orchestrate divine intervention in the world around me. But more than anything else, I want to grow more in love with You. I want to know You more deeply and follow hard after You. As I am blessed with holy moments, help me to praise You, the Holy One. Lord, be glorified in my past, my present and my future. I surrender them all into Your caring hands.

Amen.

Endnotes

Chapter 1

1. Franklin Eltman, "Holocaust Survivor Gets His Bar Mitzvah," February 7, 2006 htttp://*Newsday.com*, (accessed February 17, 2006).
2. Ibid.
3. Ibid.
4. Josh McDowell, "Love," Index #2200-2209, *Bible Illustrator for Windows*, version 3.0 F. Parson Technology, 1990-98.
5. Bill Moyers, "Take Back America," Washington D.C., Transcript from the Federal News Service, June 3, 2005, p. 9. http://www.ourfuture.org/document.cfm?documentID=1974, (accessed August 5, 2006).
6. Billy Graham, *How to Be Born Again* (Waco, TX: Word, 1977), p. 37.
7. J. Vernon McGee, *Thru the Bible—Joshua Through Psalms* (Nashville, TN: Thomas Nelson, 1982), p. 97.

Chapter 2

1. James S. Hewett, *Illustrations Unlimited* (Wheaton, IL: Tyndale House Publishers, 1988), p. 419.
2. Warren Wiersbe, *On Being a Servant of God* (Grand Rapids, MI: Baker Books, 1999), p. 60.

Chapter 3

1. Oswald Chambers, "Guidance," Index #1465-1471 *Bible Illustrator for Windows Version 3.0 F,* © 1990-98 by Parson Technology.
2. *Merriam-Webster's Dictionary*, 7th ed., s.v. "desire."
3. Dan Betzer, *Pentecostal Evangelical Leadership*, vol. 12, no. 3. http://www.witandwisdom.org/archive/20010605.htm, (accessed August 5, 2006).
4. Jan Jarvis and Robert Tharp, "A Family Shattered: Mother of 3-Day-Old Twins Faces Loss of Husband, Son," *Ft. Worth Star Telegram*, June 16, 1999, final AM edition, p. 1.
5. Jan Jarvis and Robert Tharp, "Crash Victim's Widow Tends to Newborn Twins," *Fort Worth Star Telegram*, June 17, 1999, final AM edition, p. 1.
6. D. Martyn Lloyd-Jones, "The Best of Martyn Lloyd-Jones," *Christianity Today*, vol. 38, no. 7.

Chapter 4

1. Blaine Smith, *The Yes Anxiety: Taming the Fear of Commitment* (Westmont, IL: InterVarsity Press, 1995), quoted in www.gospelcom.net.

2. Biblesoft's New Exhaustive Strong's Numbers and Concordance with Expanded Greek-Hebrew Dictionary. Copyright © 1994, Biblesoft and International Bible Translators, Inc.

3. Corrie ten Boom, with John and Elizabeth Sherrill, *The Hiding Place* (London: Hodder and Stoughton, 1976), n.p.

4. James S. Hewett, *Illustrations Unlimited* (Wheaton, IL: Tyndale House Publishers, 1988), p. 157.

5. "Providence," Index #2905-2913, *Bible Illustrator for Windows*, CD-ROM, version 3.0 F. Parson Technology, 1990-98.

6. Warren Wiersbe, *On Being a Servant of God* (Grand Rapids, MI: Baker Books, 1993), p. 72.

7. Rick Warren, *The Purpose-Driven Life* (Grand Rapids, MI: Zondervan, 2002), pp. 174-175.

Chapter 5

1. "Faith," *The New Unger's Bible Dictionary* (Chicago, IL: Moody Press, 1988), n.p.

2. "Trust," Index #1214-1218, *Bible Illustrator for Windows*, CD-ROM, version 3.0 F. Parson Technology, 1990-98.

3. Oswald Chambers, quoted in Edythe Draper, *Draper's Book of Quotations for the Christian World* (Wheaton, IL: Tyndale House Publishers, 1992), entries 11484-11487.

4. D. Elton Trueblood, *Men of Integrity*, vol. 1, no. 2, Bible Illustrator; also see Croft M. Pentz, *The Complete Book of Zingers* (Wheaton: Tyndale House Publishers, 1990), n.p.

5. D. Martyn Lloyd-Jones, *Christian Reader*, vol. 31; Edythe Draper, *Draper's Book of Quotations for the Christian World* (Wheaton, IL: Tyndale House Publishers, 1992), entries 3676-3679.

6. Abraham Lincoln, *Christian Reader*, vol. 33, no. 2, Edythe Draper, *Draper's Book of Quotations for the Christian World* (Wheaton, IL: Tyndale House Publishers, 1992), entries 3688-3691.

7. *Vine's Expository Dictionary of Biblical Words* (Nashville, TN: Thomas Nelson Publishers, 1985), n.p.

8. Adapted from Franklin Graham, *Rebel with a Cause* (Nashville, TN: Thomas Nelson Publishers, 1995), pp. 13-34.

9. Elisabeth Elliot, *Keep a Quiet Heart* (Ann Arbor, MI: Vine Books, 1995), n.p. Barbara and David P. Mikkelson, "The Ant and the Contact Lens, 08/22/05. http://www.snopes.com (accessed January 17, 2006).

10. Jerry Bridges, *Trusting God* (Colorado Springs, CO: NavPress, 1988), p. 203.

11. Source unknown.

12. Philip Bennett Power, *The "I Wills" of the Psalms* (Edinburgh: The Banner of Truth Trust, 1985), p. 63.

13. Charles West. http://en.thinkexist.com/quotes/charles_c._west/ (accessed August 8, 2006)

Chapter 6

1. *Merriam-Webster's Collegiate Dictionary,* 11th edition, p. 1001.
2. Adam Clarke's Commentary, Electronic Database, copyright © 1996 by Biblesoft.
3. Barnes' Notes, Electronic Database, copyright © 1997 by Biblesoft
4. Jamieson, Fausset, and Brown Commentary, Electronic Database, copyright © 1997 by Biblesoft.
5. Keil & Delitzsch, Commentary on the Old Testament: New Updated Edition, Electronic Database, copyright © 1996 by Hendrickson Publishers, Inc.
6. Ibid.
7. Adapted from Merlin S. Berry, "History of Northeastern North Carolina Storms, 1998-2002." http://www.rootsweb.com (accessed January 20, 2006).
8. Adapted from Keith C. Heidorn, *The Weather Doctor's Book Review,* September 15, 1999. http://www.islandnet.com (accessed January 6, 2006).
9. Gregory Asimakoupoulos, *Leadership,* vol. 6, no. 4.
10. Oswald Chambers, *My Utmost for His Highest.*

Make the Most of Every Moment

Some women seem to be born with a joyful outlook. Others have to work at it. But joy can be a part of any woman's life, regardless of the circumstances. What does it take to live a life of joy? It starts with "doing good" toward one's self as well as others, taking care of physical and mental needs in a way that sparks well-being and happiness, tending to those areas of life that challenge us—even when we don't feel like it—without complaining, and ending each day with thanksgiving. *Squeeze the Moment* shows you how to look at your life in a fresh way and to squeeze your moments—the happy ones, the tragic ones, the predictable and unexpected ones—for all they're worth. Those who do are sure to find the treasure that each moment contains

Squeeze the Moment
Making the Most of Life's Gifts and Challenges
Karen O'Connor
ISBN 08307.38363

Regal
God's Word for Your World™

Inspiring Reading for Women

Moments Together for Couples
Daily Devotions for Drawing Near to God and One Another
Dennis and Barbara Rainey
ISBN 08307.17544

Release the Pain, Embrace the Joy
Help for the Hurting Heart
Michelle McKinney Hammond
ISBN 08307.37227

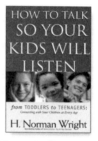

How to Talk So Your Kids Will Listen
From Toddlers to Teenagers—Connecting with Your Children at Every Age
H. Norman Wright
ISBN 08307.33280

Always Daddy's Girl
Understanding Your Father's Impact on Who You Are
H. Norman Wright
ISBN 08307.27620

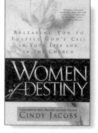

Women of Destiny
Releasing You to Fulfill God's Call in Your Life and in the Church
Cindy Jacobs
ISBN 08307.18648

The Measure of a Woman
What Really Makes a Woman Beautiful
Gene A. Getz with Elaine Getz
ISBN 08307.32861